188

52

178

22

60

82

66

112

94

148 & 186

199

102

90

194

181

66

174

169

124

56

66

166

86

24

188

19

206

108

Contents

Hello again!

It's been 2 years since *The Purl Stitch*. I hope you've been busy—exploring your mastery of and interest in knitting! I've been busy—thinking through, designing, and knitting the garments that I think offer what you might want to know about color.

Color is a very powerful concept. First, there are the 'rules' of color, the 'how' of putting colors together. This whole subject is intimidating to some, wonderfully exciting to others. While there is no end to the possibilities of color combining, I think a few simple concepts help us move from the first category to the second.

The greater number of puzzle pieces are the techniques available with which to do this color work. There are so many, they are so various, and they are wonderfully satisfying to master. It is to these skills that the patterns of the book are dedicated.

The designs in this book are like those in *Knit* and *Purl:* some simple, some classic, some unexpected. I have continued to design with the same aesthetic that has inspired me from the beginning. There's really no mystery here: the pieces are what my 27-year-old daughter or I would like to wear. Sometimes she surprises me, wanting the pieces that were planned for my age group. And sometimes I'm thrilled to find that my friends and I can wear the pieces I thought were for the younger crowd.

So, here's my take on *Color!* I hope it inspires you, teaches you, and brings you a few surprises of your own. Because color is a lovely and thrilling subject. And in the words of one of my favorite songs... "I see trees of green, red roses too; I see them bloom, for me and you. And I think to myself, what a wonderful world."

How to work with *Color*

This book assumes a basic ability to knit and purl. Yes, there are garments with very few skills required. But the lengthy descriptions of these skills are not in this book. What is here is a Skills-at-a-glance section (see page 228), a refresher course for basic skills. For a true beginner, please consider learning the basics first.

But once you do have these skills, here's how you may work with this book.

1 Look through the pages to feel inspired. Look at, but do not be distracted by, the colors of the garments. If you like the colors in which it is shown, then proceed, If you think you like something, but not its color, take a black and white photocopy of it. If you still like it, then proceed.

2 Check out the pattern's difficulty level (described at the top of the vitals column, see page 15). This will help you determine if you are ready to make this piece—or to learn what you need to make this piece.

3 Look at the italicized note after the garment introduction. It tells you what colors were used. If you encounter any color terms with which you are not familiar, go to the Working with Color chapter (page 3). (If I think it helpful, I'll direct you to a particular page in this chapter.)

4 Now go to the yarn shop and find the colors that best describe your vision. Be prepared to be flexible: again, the Working with Color section will help.

5 If you need it, This Book At–a–Glance (page 14) is a quick reference to help you through your purchases and your pattern.

6 As you work through the pattern, here's how the instructions work. If a skill is needed, and addressed in Skills-at-a-Glance, you are told this in the notes at the beginning of the pattern. (And there might be other helpful information in these notes.) If a skill is needed that is elaborated in this book, a page reference is given the first time the skill is used in the pattern.

7 Finishing skills (seaming, how to pick up around a neckline, etc.) were elaborated in detail in *The Purl Stitch* but do not appear here. You might need to refer to *Purl* or some other reference for finishing skills. (You'll never regret attention paid to this part of your work.)

8 So, be brave (Don't let color scare you!), have fun, and perhaps get warmed up and ready by reading Seeing Color (page 1).

SEEING COLOR

Does this sound familiar? You holiday, buy an outfit, come home, look in a mirror, and wonder "What was I thinking?!" Or have you questioned why we wear black to funerals? And have you ever noticed that little girls of 9 all love purple?

What this tells us is that color is simply not an absolute: even those of us without any symptoms of color blindness have our perception of color changed—with geography, with mood, with seasons, with age. There are times when your vision, even your judgment, is altered by factors outside your eye's receptivity.

Light is one of these factors. In bright and direct light, colors are washed out. This means that in those climes where we most like to holiday—the tropics, with its directly-overhead, full sun—people wear bright colors. Darker and duller colors would disappear in this light.

So, there's a reason people in Hawaii wear those famously bright shirts: they can see them! And there's a reason we look with wonderment when they're worn in more northerly climes. Similarly, people who live in darker, duller climes (with low light, or a cloud-obscured sun) wear duller colors. And seasons can have a similar effect: summer = bright sun; winter = low light. We dress accordingly.

What this suggests, other than to be very careful buying clothes when traveling, is that if we wish to take a photograph of something colorful (and aren't professionals with scrims, filters, light meters, options for exposure), we should take the picture early in the morning, late in the afternoon, in shadow, or under clouds.

Mood also affects our ability to see color. When we are grieving, we cannot see it accurately. I remember, after my husband died, thinking I looked like a clown in anything other than very dark colors. This might explain why those who are in mourning wear either black or white. Yes, it's a sign of respect; and yes, it gives information. But I believe its roots are in a physical reality, and I find that pretty amazing!

Age, too, affects our ability to see color. Babies are born with under-developed color cones and at first can only see black and white. They quickly graduate to the primaries: blue, red, yellow. (Babies simply do not see the pastel sweaters they are wearing, but we've probably not made them for the babies anyway?) As they age, and their color cones mature, they're able to see the secondaries— colors produced by mixing primaries. So, little girls between perhaps 6 and 11 love purple. Boys of the same age love orange and green.

Eventually humans develop the ability to see tertiary colors: those produced by mixing a primary with a secondary. As fully-formed adults we love those colors that can only be described with more than one word (unless the color has a name all its own, like chartreuse). As mature and sophisticated adults, we love blue-purple, plum purple, eggplant purple, something other than just purple. So, go find *your* purple, and have fun!

WORKING WITH COLOR

Think of the power color has. When we see someone's wonderful, newly-knit sweater, our first impression is of color. We are aware of its yarn and stitch pattern and silhouette, but the first thing we notice, mention, remember is its color.

So, given its power, color has the potential to scare us. Why else would 80% of knitters insist upon knitting the garment in the exact color in which it is shown? That's a huge testament to the power of color—that we can't imagine it in another color so we bypass the garment if it isn't knit in a color that appeals to us.

How to overcome our fear of color's power? It's not easy! Sometimes the richness of the environment is the problem. We walk into a yarn shop and are assaulted by possibilities. Or we read a color book and are overwhelmed by theories, rules, and pages and pages of suggestions. On the other hand, sometimes the limitations of the environment is the problem. We know we need a particular color, but the yarn we like is just not available in anything close to that color. What to do?

What I offer here are basic and simple rules, meant to give you safe decisions when faced with lots of choices. And yes, even with my suggestions in hand, you will find yourself in a situation where exactly the right green is not available; what follows should help you make the best choice in that situation also.

Of course there are people who approach color differently. And of course there are more complex rules, theories, discussions, suggestions about color in other books. Every approach has validity. We are, after all, talking about one of the wonders of our world! What I offer is a starting point for those who want to gain confidence. With that in hand, color's power will become something to embrace, to explore, to enhance your love of knitting.

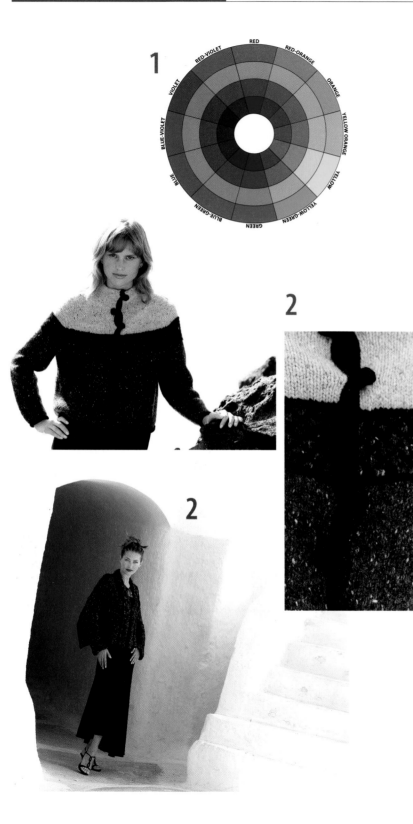

Working with color

Before discussing color-combining, there are two aspects of color we need to appreciate: undertones, and color demands.

1 **UNDERTONES**
In what follows I talk about colors—even neutrals—as warm or cool or balanced. Look at a color wheel to see these qualities. The colors from blue-green to red-violet are cool (more blue than yellow). The colors from yellow-green to red-orange are warm (more yellow than blue). And red and green sit on the boundary, so are 'balanced.'

DEMANDING COLORS
Here is what demands the eye's attention:
- the lightest color (white before anything else);
- the warmest color (yellow before violet);
- the brightest or clearest color (vivid blue before gray-blue or dark-blue).

Neutrals
For a garment that might never go out of style, these are worth consideration.

BLACK, GRAY, WHITE
The least-complicated neutrals are black, gray, and white. And while black is pretty much just black, gray can be more complex (charcoal, medium gray, pale gray, silver), as can white (off-, winter, stone).

2 Use a critical eye to look for warm or cool undertones. Is there a lot of blue in the gray, or is it yellow-based? Or is it neither? The same applies to white: is it cool, warm, or balanced? Once you've established this, it's a safe choice to mix cool neutrals with other cool neutrals or warm neutrals with other warm neutrals. And balanced neutrals can probably go both ways. But do be careful with whites: some whites can make other whites look dirty.

3

4

BROWN, BEIGE, TAUPE, PEWTER, BRONZE **3**

Although these are actually complex colors, we can think of them as neutrals. And they will have the same warm or cool or balanced undertones. Again, a safe choice is to combine all warm or all cool: a cool chocolate brown + a cool taupe, a warm chestnut brown + a warm beige.

DARK COLORS **4**

Brown really is just a dark yellow, orange, or red. So it helps to see other dark colors—any version of dark blue, dark green, or dark violet (as shown to right)—as neutral, rather than struggling with them as a color. It's never *wrong* to think of darks in terms of their color. I'm just suggesting that you have the choice—to see navy as a dark-enough blue to be treated as black or gray or any other dark neutral.

6

5

7

Neutrals and color

5 It's easy and generally successful to combine a neutral with a color. And if the color is warm, then the neutral should be; if the color is cool, then the neutral

6 should be. But, really, you can put just about anything with a balanced gray because it is so un-demanding.

7 Adding more neutrals is no more difficult, but the complexity of the finished piece is heightened considerably. Just bring the same issues and decisions to bear: if the color is cool or warm, then choose similar neutrals. (Again, balanced neutrals can 'go both ways.')

Variegateds

At the other end of the spectrum from neutrals might be variegated yarns—yarns with many colors dyed into them.

RELATED VARIEGATEDS

An easy way to work with variegateds is to find others that relate then go play! Find your predominant color, then add anything with the same predominant color. If some have flecks of other colors, that might be exciting—might make the combination less 'ho hum.'

There are ways to check out, help, or ensure the success of a combination: see Integration, page 12. And read more about variegated yarns in Chapter 1 (page 42).

VARIEGATED + 1 NEUTRAL

Variegated yarns are wonderful with a neutral. Look at the variegated to see if the majority of the colors are cool or warm: if there are many colors, it's probably balanced. Now pick a neutral with the same undertones.

VARIEGATED + 1 COLOR

To knit a variegated with a solid, pick a color that never quite appears in the variegated: otherwise, you'll get spots where the variegated disappears. A darker solid color (even if only slightly darker) will set off the variegated best.

8

8

8

9

10

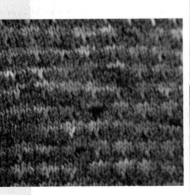

9

10

11

11   To use a solid as an accent, look at the combination from 2 feet away. What looks good close up may be overpowering and not attractive from a distance.

Color theory

I hope you don't approach color theory assuming it has to be difficult. With the simplest understanding of a color wheel and a few basic principles, safe choices abound!

12

THE COLOR WHEEL

This common color wheel has concentric rings with the 12 basic colors. Look at them at their brightest—the labelled, outside ring. First the 3 primaries: red, yellow, blue. Next the 3 secondaries: orange, green, violet (produced by mixing 2 primaries). Finally the 6 tertiaries: colors with 2 names and that appear in every alternate segment (produced by mixing the adjacent primary + secondary).

A color wheel is a valuable tool…not just because it's pretty and helps us understand color. You will use it to produce color combinations that appeal to you. Here's how:

- study successful color combinations and plot them onto a color wheel;
- record the formation you see;
- keep the formation, but move it to other positions on the wheel, until you see other combinations you like.

TONAL RANGES

The concentric rings (usually 4) are *tonal ranges*. In colors that sit in the same tonal range you should see the following.

- The brights are simply pure colors (without white or gray or black): see vivid.
- The tints are pure colors+white: see pale or pastel.
- The tones are pure colors+gray: see dusty.
- The shades are pure colors+black: see dark.

13

14

Color combinations guaranteed to succeed are from the same tonal range. So it's important to see these clearly as you consider combinations. Do the colors have the same vividness (if brights)? Do they have the same crisp, prettiness (if tints)? Do they have the same darkness (if shades)? Or do they have the same dusty quality (if tones)? (The striped garment to left seems a mix of light and dark, but they're all tones and so combine well.) Having said all this, do not be a slave to this concept. Sometimes a slight variation in tonal range provides interest (see the man's sweater below). And see Breaking the rules, page 12.

How do you know to what tonal range a yarn belongs? A color is best understood in relation to another. For example, look at the 'mystery' color beside one you know to be a tint, a tone, a vivid, or a shade. Side by side, they usually reveal themselves.

A MIX OF TONAL RANGES / DARK + LIGHT

Many traditional patterns are based upon an interplay of light and dark. And if we combine light and dark, we draw the eye to the lighter area. Sometimes, that is exactly what we want to do.

HALF OF THE COLOR WHEEL

One way to work with color is to say "I like all warm!" Good for you! Go find your side of the color wheel and play! But consider what follows.

13

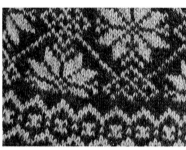

14

14

15

15

15

**Experience the Color Wheel: go to Web Features at
www.knittinguniverse.com**

16

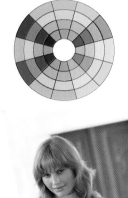

16 **ANALOGOUS COLORS**
Analogous colors are separated by one segment on a color wheel. Two analogous colors often make a more successful combination than 2 side-by-side colors. (And here's a cool trick. If you need red but can't find it, use red-orange and red-violet: your eye will 'see' red!)

17 Another nice 2-color combo is 2 colors separated by 2 segments.

18 And a nice 3-color combo is 2 adjacent colors+1 analogous color. (Do you see that skipping a segment leads to more interesting combinations?)

17

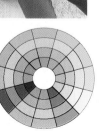

18

COMPLEMENTARY COLORS

Complementary colors sit directly opposite on the color wheel: the complement to violet is yellow, and the complement to a group is the color that sits opposite the center of the group.

The thing to know about a complementary is that the eye wants to see it. If you look at white dots on a violet field, the white turns to the complementary—to yellow (which is why you can only wear that white and violet sweater with off-white pants). Gray is similarly affected.

But do we always give the eye what it wants? Certainly not! (What would the world be like if everybody got what they thought they wanted?) I might use a complementary if any of the following apply:
- if I need it (to keep a white or a gray clear),
- if it's a color I like (a lot),
- if it's a color that will match something I want to wear with the piece,
- if it's a balanced or cool color,
- if the color and the complementary are equally demanding.

SPLIT COMPLEMENTARIES

Another way to add a complementary is to split it—by using the 2 colors on either side of the complementary.

TRIADS

The eye likes to see both sides of the color wheel—in a straight line (complementary) or a skinny triangle (split complementary). So it's not a stretch to go for a wider triangle: a triad. (The garment to the right shows both a triad—the wider triangle—plus a split complementary—the narrower triangle.)

19

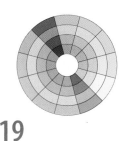

19

19

20

20

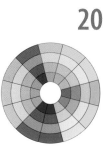

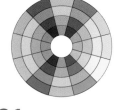

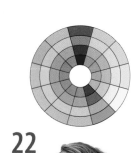

21

22

21 TETRADS
After seeing complementaries split into skinny and then wider triangles, it's not a big leap to go from triangles to squares: to a tetrad (which you could also see as pair of analogous colors).

Breaking the rules
We all know that rules are meant to be broken. But how do we break the rules successfully?

22 WHEN CLOSE ENOUGH IS GOOD ENOUGH
Some times we can't quite find the complement. The color right next door is a safe choice.

23 INTEGRATION
Think of integration as blending things together. It can make a breaking-the-rules color combination work—by the yarn itself (like the striped lace garment, which has yarns that are cool plus warm plus a mixture) or by working more than one yarn at a time (as in the poncho), or with a color pattern (of lots of tiny stripes), or with a stitch pattern (as in Chapter 3).

23

23

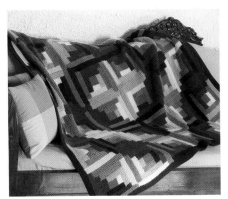

24

INSPIRATION FROM OTHER SOURCES

If you see something you love—a piece of art, fabric, flooring—and you love its colors, then go for it! Get as close as you can to its colors, paying close attention to how much of each was used.

24 Cynthia's Afghan is based upon a traditional quilt block: darks+lights+warm center. Staying within a tonal range doesn't happen!

The Knitting Bag Jacket was based upon, guess what...a favorite knitting bag. The original mixed tonal ranges and the colors pretty much cover the whole color wheel. Integration is at work to make this combination succeed.

25

25 Sometimes we get a glimpse of something, and we choose colors based on an ephemeral image. But our memory is suspect, and we can't find all the colors anyway. And though we wish to follow color principles, the original didn't seem to. Image in mind, we soldier on.

26 This is what happened with the Color-party Parka. I had seen something but could neither remember nor find the colors of the original. And I certainly didn't follow the tonal ranges rule. But when I plotted its color on a color wheel, I found 4 pairs of side-by-side colors. Cool!

As suggested earlier, when you find color combinations you like, try plotting them on the wheel. You'll learn a lot—the rules and perhaps how to break them. And whether you use these principles or discover your own, I hope you experiment with and take joy in the world of color that awaits.

26

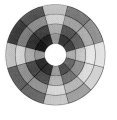

This Book At-a-Glance

The story
about this pattern

Color Notes
(to describe color
choices—often
with references to a
discussion in Working
with Color)

Other Notes
(often about sizing or
yarn or gauge)

The vitals
(see facing page)

The yarn I used,
and how much of it, to
knit the size shown in
the photo

Pattern Notes
(to offer special instructions and to
mention skills that will be required
and for which a quick reference
can be found in Skills-at-a-Glance,
page 228)

The pattern instructions
Common abbreviations are used.
For a quick reference to terms and
abbreviations, see the Glossary, pages 226–227.

The first time a new skill is used in
a pattern, it will appear like this:
see Knitting with 2 colors, page 152.

Additional skills
New skills are
found at the end of
each chapter

Fixing mistakes
Common mistakes are anticipated:
the remedies are in the Oops! chapter.
As you knit a pattern, check out pages
224–225.

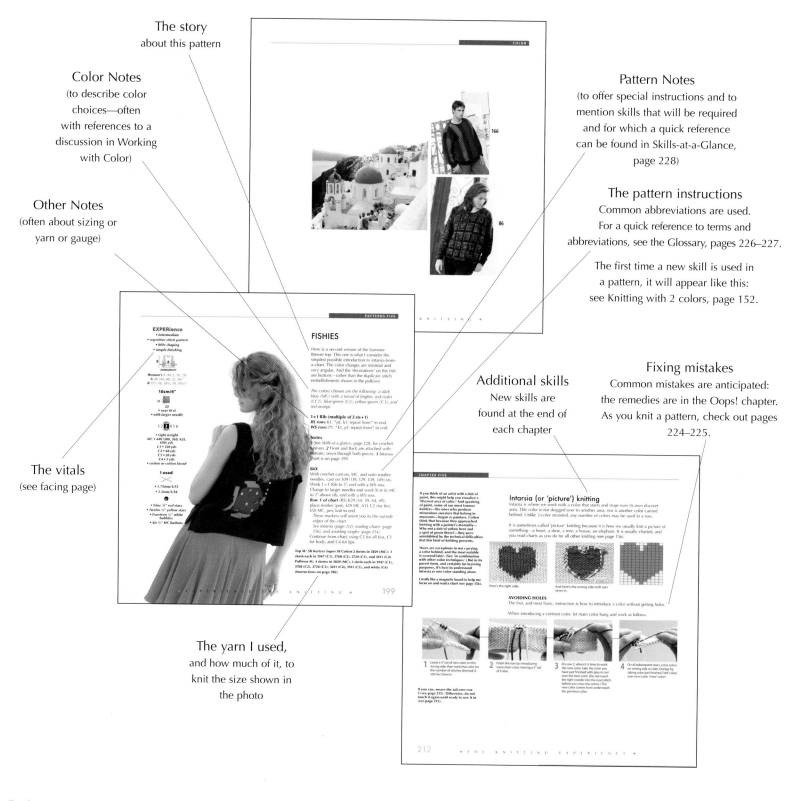

EXPERIence

- *intermediate*
- *repetitive stitch pattern*
- *mid-level shaping*
- *mid-level finishing*

C

B **A**

LOOSE FIT

Woman's S (M, L, 1X, 2X)

A 39 (42, 46, 50, 54)"
B 28 (28, 28, 29, 29)"
C 28 (28, 28, 29, 29)"

10cm/4"

28 ▦ *17*

- *over 3-Block stitch pattern*
- *using larger needles*
- *after blocking*

You'll need

1 2 3 **4** 5 6

- *Medium weight*
- *1090 (1220, 1300, 1380, 1470) yds*
- *wool blend*

I used

✕

- *4.5mm/US7*
- *4mm/US6*

☻

two 19mm/¾"

Skill level The more capital letters, the more skills required.

Fit describes how closely the garment will fit your body.

Sizes in which the pattern is offered.

Garment measurements as they correspond to the A, B, C lines on the fit icon.

Gauge The number of stitches you should have in 10cm or 4".

Stitch pattern The kind of stitches you should use for your gauge swatch and how it should be treated.

Yarn weight The category of yarn recommended.

Yarn amount The number of yards you'll need.

Yarn type Specific suggestions may be offered.

Type of needles Straight, unless circular or double-pointed are recommended.

Needle size The size I used to obtain gauge.

Buttons or other notions, if required.

The vitals column that accompanies every pattern is loaded with information, replacing a whole lot of words that can make knitting patterns look like no-fun text books. I think these icons are more knitter-friendly. But their most important function may be to make knitting a universal language.

For more information on fit, sizing, measurements, yarn, needles, and for conversion charts, see pages 234–235. For an expanded discussion of this material, see *The Knit Stitch* or *The Purl Stitch*, 'The Choices We Make.'

LET THE YARN DO THE WORK

What better way to deal with color's power than just, well, let someone else do the work? Like those wonderful people who produce yarns of many colors. Right. Why not just pick variegated yarns? Good idea.

I remember 10 years ago when I first went to the United States to teach at a Stitches conference. I walked into the market and was absolutely stunned at the array of variegated yarns. (It was rather like the reaction we hear from people when they first come to North American grocery stores. They cannot imagine having so many choices! They wonder if we know how lucky we are.)

Well, back then so many choices in variegated yarns were not readily available. I looked at the cacophony of color and thought, "Where do I start? What does one do with this stuff?"

Variegated yarns are everywhere now, and I have more experience with them. But many knitters don't. How do they walk into a yarn shop and imagine this stuff in anything more than a scarf?

This chapter explores a few options with variegated yarns: how to use them, how maybe to not use them, how to produce your own, how to do nifty things with scarves. These are small steps you can take into a big and beautiful world. Then you'll find your own way to play in that world. And it is lucky we are to have it!

(For a fun and simple way to play with 3 variegated yarns, check out the Yarn-Party Scarf. This 1-row-in-each version of the Shaped Scarf from *The Knit Stitch* is available as a free download at **www.knittinguniverse.com**.)

Faith jacket
Adult's S–M, Bulky weight: MANOS DEL URUGUAY 100% Wool
6 skeins in 104 (A), 3 skeins in 112 (B), 1 skein in M

Adult's: 3 balls each
LANA GROSSA Telaio Print in 402 (A) and STACY CHARLES Baci in 36 (B); 1
ball each TRENDSETTER Blossom in 19 (C), STACY CHARLES Twist in 5 (D),
and TRENDSETTER Shadow Metal in 103 (E); 2 balls each TRENDSETTER
Flora in 1040 (F), Papi in 23 (G), and Flora in 22 (H); 1 ball each CRYSTAL
PALACE Squiggles in 9296 (I) and ROWAN Summer Tweed in 537 (K)

THE EXPERIENCE

EXperience
- *very easy*
- *simple finishing*

Child's 4–6 (10–12, Adult's)
- *measurements on page 20*

10cm/4"

8
10
- *over garter stitches and ridges (knit every row) using 2 strands of yarn (1 bulky + 1 fine) held together*
- *before blocking*

You'll need

1 **2** 3 4 5 6

- **Fine weight**
- total of 320 (400, 520) yds
- novelty yarns

1 2 3 4 **5-6**

- **Bulky, or Super Bulky**
- total of 320 (400, 520) yds
- novelty yarns
&
Bulky weight
K • 30 (40, 50) yds
coordinating color, for assembling

I used

- **9mm/US13**

- **6mm/J**

Child´s 4–6: 3 balls each
ESTELLE Dazzle in 1196 (A) and TRENDSETTER Dune in 36
(B); 1 ball SKACEL Sizzle in 4148 (C); 3 balls TRENDSETTER
Shadow Metal in 103 (D), 1 ball Flora in 1040 (E), 2 balls Flora
in 22 (F), and 1 ball Viola Print in 14 (G)

YARN-PARTY PONCHO

Over the past few years, I have been told by yarn shop owners of the tremendous number of their customers who only knit scarves. So, I thought it appropriate to see what could be done with scarves. This result is one of my favorite pieces of knitting.

Its title has a bit of a story. I originally thought of it as the 8-scarf poncho: very descriptive, not very imaginative. But when I wore the red one, I found myself singing 'I am a wild party.' Hence, the yarn-party poncho!

Novelty yarns can be difficult to handle, and you might need a needle size different than the one I used. While gauge is approximate, do make a gauge swatch, and read the note at the end of the scarves section.

While there are 8 scarves, each with 2 yarns, this does not mean that you need to purchase 16 different yarns. In fact, the piece works better if you don't. Find 3–6 heavier (weight 5 or 6) yarns with a predominant color, and buy enough yardage. Then find some number of lighter (weight 2) yarns of similar color, and buy enough yardage. Now mix and match the lighter with heavier. This mixture and repetition of yarns help the colors integrate.

Don't worry if you find a yarn you like and it doesn't have the yardage needed. Much of the yarn goes into the scarves, but some goes into the fringe. If you run short, you'll just put less of that yarn into the fringe.

Notes
1 See *Skills-at-a-glance*, page 228, for e-wrap cast-on, and attaching fringe. **2** Gauge and final measurements are approximate.

SCARVES (MAKE 8)
See schematic for suggested yarn arrangements. With one strand of Fine yarn and one strand of Bulky or Super Bulky held together, e-wrap cast on 8 (9, 10) sts, leaving 5 (6, 8)" tail.

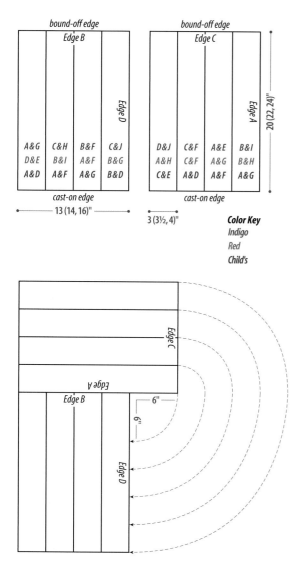

bound-off edge

Edge B			
			Edge D
A&G	C&H	B&F	C&J
D&E	B&I	A&F	B&G
A&D	A&F	A&G	B&D

cast-on edge

◄—— 13 (14, 16)" ——►

bound-off edge

Edge C			
			Edge A
D&J	C&F	A&E	B&I
A&H	C&F	A&G	B&H
C&E	A&D	A&F	A&G

cast-on edge

3 (3½, 4)"

20 (22, 24)"

Color Key
Indigo
Red
Child's

Edge C

Edge A

Edge B

Edge D

6"

6"

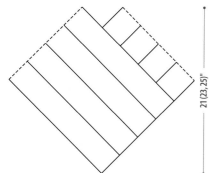

21 (23, 25)"

Knit 80 (88, 96) rows—40 (44, 48) ridges.
Average length is 20 (22, 24)".
  Some of the pieces will be narrower and longer than others. Just make sure that when you begin the piece it is approximately 3 (3½, 4)" wide, then don't worry how it hangs when you've knit the full length. The assembling and blocking will bring it all together.
Bind off loosely, leaving 5 (6, 8)" tail.

FINISHING
Make 2 rectangles
With crochet hook and 1 strand K, join 4 scarves with single crochet (sc) to form one side of poncho (see diagram for arrangement) as follows:
Place 2 scarves with wrong sides together. Begin at cast-on edges, leave 5 (6, 8)" tail (to incorporate into fringe). Work sc loosely, through both pieces in spaces between garter ridges (see page 44). Continue until 4 scarves are joined.
Join other 4 scarves in same way.

Join rectangles
Join edge A to edge B as follows: *sc 1 bound-off st to 1 space between garter ridges 6 (7, 8) times, skip 1 st; repeat from*.
  You are seaming 32 (36, 40) sts to 28 (32, 36) ridges.
Join edge C to edge D in same way.
  Neck will be 6" wide at rest but wider when worn.

Fringe
Wrap yarns around 5 (6, 8)" book, and cut to make pieces 10 (12, 16)" long.
  You will need 288 (320, 352) pieces of yarn for fringe. Try to use equal amounts of all the yarns, although you will run out of some sooner than others.
Attach 4 randomly-chosen pieces of yarn at every 2nd st or alternate space between garter ridges around entire lower edge; include tails into fringe as you encounter them. Trim fringe.
Sew in any remaining tails.
  There is no right or wrong side to the finished piece, sew in tails invisibly.

Blocking
Soak garment in Eucalan or in water with small amount of hair conditioner or fabric softener. Rinse minimally or not at all.
Squeeze out excess moisture. Lay flat to dry.
  Blocking makes it drape well. Do not worry if it doesn't dry symmetrically: it's not supposed to.

Adult's: 2 balls each TRENDSETTER
Quadro in 5966 (A), Liberty in 121 (B), Aquarius in 819 (C); 1 ball each
Checkmate in 1039 (D), Joy in 1191 (E), Viola Print in 26 (F), Papi in 18 (G),
Metal in 31 (H) and 54 (I), Aura in 26 (J); small amount of coordinating color (K)

EXPerience
- *easy*
- *repetitive stitch pattern*
- *no shaping*
- *little finishing*

OVERSIZED FIT

S (M, L, 1X, 2X)
A 40 (44, 48, 52, 56)"
buttoned
B 16½ (17, 17½, 18, 18½)"

10cm/4"

40

20

- *over Garter Slip pattern*
- *using larger needles*

You'll need

1 2 3 **4** 5 6

- *Medium weight*
- *660 (750, 840, 940, 1040) yds*
- *cotton or cotton blend*

I used

- *4.5mm/US7*
- *3.75mm/US5*

- *4mm/G*

☺

- *six 19mm/¾"*

SUMMER BREEZE

I modeled this top on my favorite, and oldest, summer dress. You will see another version of it later in the book, but this one is easier and done with variegated yarn.

The yarn used is a medium-color-change variegated. See page 40 to read about this yarn and how to avoid, if you wish, the color stacking that appears here.

Garter Slip (multiple of 5 sts + 1)
Right-side rows Knit.
Wrong-side rows *With yarn in front, slip first st purlwise (sl 1), k4; repeat from* to last st, sl 1.

NOTES
1 See *Skills-at-a-glance*, page 228, for crochet cast-on and slip stitches. **2** Front and Back are joined with buttons sewn through both pieces.

FRONT/BACK (MAKE 2)
With crochet cast-on and onto larger needle, cast on 106 (116, 126, 136, 146) sts.
Work Garter Slip until piece measures 12½ (13, 13½, 14, 14½)", end with a WS row.
Bind off.

LEFT STRAP
Designate one piece as the Front. Turn to WS.
*Measure 4 (5, 6, 7, 8)" from left edge, then find 4th garter ridge from top.
With smaller needle, working from left to right, slip needle through next 16 stitch bumps. Knit each stitch—16 sts. Turn.
Work Garter Slip over these 16 sts until strap measures 8".
The strap will stretch with wearing. Stretch vigorously before measuring.
Bind off.
Sew strap to WS of Back, 4 (5, 6, 7, 8)" from left edge and 4 ridges from top.

RIGHT STRAP
Turn Back to WS, work as for Left Strap from* to end, sewing strap to WS of Front.

FINISHING
Sew both straps at bound-off edges of Front and Back to secure.
Join sides with buttons as follows:
With WS of Front and Back together, and Front facing, sew a button through both layers, approximately 3" from top at side.
Sew a button at same place on other side of Front.
Try the garment on to be sure the button is high enough for modesty. Move buttons, if needed.
Sew next pair of buttons approximately 3" from lower edge and final pair of buttons centered between others.

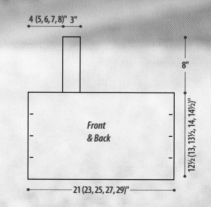

4 (5, 6, 7, 8)" 3"

8"

12½ (13, 13½, 14, 14½)"

Front & Back

21 (23, 25, 27, 29)"

M: 9 skeins BERROCO Cotton Twist in 8464 Morandi Mix

EXPerience
- *easy*
- *simple shaping*
- *lots of finishing*

OVERSIZED FIT

Child's 2–4 (8–10)
[Adult's S–M (L–1X, 2X+)]

A *31 (45) [59 (63, 67)]"*
B *14 (17) [20 (21, 22)]"*
C *17½ (23) [29 (30, 31)]"*

Child's, Bulky, Medium
10cm/4"

24
14
16

24, 14, 18

- *over garter stitches and ridges (knit every row)*
- *after steam pressing or blocking, if needed*

You'll need

2 OR **4** OR **5**

- *Fine weight*
- *3 yarns*
- *350 (525) yds each*
- *Medium weight*
- *1700 (1900, 2100) yds*

OR

- *Bulky weight*
- *1015 (1140, 1270) yds*
- *variegated or multicolor*

&

- *130 (150) yds of similar weight and coordinating color, for assembling*

Vitals continue on page 26

FAITH JACKET

This piece is very easy yet has a timeless, ageless, multi-cultural appeal. That is one reason it's the 'Faith' jacket—because it shares features with liturgical garments of all ages and cultures. But it's also the Faith jacket because you will, faithfully, knit 15 strips that won't look at all like a garment until it's assembled and sleeves are added. Sometimes, in knitting and in life, the pieces don't reveal the whole, ... but faith is rewarded!

Choose a yarn with weight. If you find a yarn that doesn't seem weighty, knit it to a tighter gauge than the label suggests. (I did this with the black and silver ribbon version.) Finish by pressing or blocking well.

The child's is worked in 3 colorways, 1 row of each (see page 42). The woman's brown version is worked in 2 colorways, 1 row A, 1 row from another ball A, 1 row B. Or, you may work all in one colorway.

NOTES
1 See *Skills-at-a-glance*, page 228, for e-wrap cast-on, slip stitches, kf&b, and eyelet buttonhole. **2** Use e-wrap cast-on throughout. **3** Stitch numbers for Child's size are given in red; numbers for Adult's sizes follow, with those for bulky yarn in blue, then medium yarn in green. If 1 set of numbers applies for adult's, it is in black.

Garter Stitch with Slip-Stitch Edge
All rows With yarn in front, slip first st purlwise (sl 1), knit (k) to end.

STRIPS 1–12
Cast on 14 (19) or 15 (16, 17) or 18 (20, 22) sts. Knit 1 row.
Work Garter Stitch with Slip-stitch Edge until piece measures 14 (17) or 20 (21, 22)", end with a wrong-side (WS) row.

Adult's S–M, Medium weight: 16 balls ESTELLE Dazzle in 306, 2 balls BERROCO Zen in 8253

Let piece hang from needle to get an accurate length measurement.

Heavier yarns may stretch up to 3" when hung.

SHORTEN OR LENGTHEN HERE

Bind off loosely.

After measuring first strip, count ridges; work 11 more strips to that number of ridges.

If you work to the gauge indicated, this will be 84 (102) or 70 (74, 77) or 80 (84, 88) ridges.

Every 3 or 4 strips, go to Finishing and do Steps 1–2.

Assemble as you go to avoid repetitive strain of crocheting all strips at once.

STRIP 13 (CENTER BACK)

Cast on 23 (27) or 21 (23, 25) or 26 (28, 30) sts.

Work to same number of ridges as Strip 1.

Do Finishing Step 3.

STRIP 14 (RIGHT FRONT)

Work as Strip 13 EXCEPT 12 (15) or 13 (14, 15) or 15 (16, 17) ridges longer.

End with a WS row, then put sts on hold.

Do Finishing Step 4.

STRIP 15 (LEFT FRONT)

Work as Strip 13 until piece measures 13".

Eyelet buttonhole, Next row (RS) Work 11 (13) or 11 (12, 13) or 13 (14, 15) sts, yarn over (yo), k2tog, knit to end.

Continue until 1 row shorter than Strip 14.

Put sts on hold.

Do Finishing Steps 5–7.

SLEEVES (MAKE 2)

If you want more control over how the color moves in the garment, see page 40. The slip stitch at the edge will be affected by this maneuver, but it will be covered by the crochet assembly.

Cast on 36 (40) or 36 (38, 40) or 44 (46, 48) sts.

Work 7 rows in Garter Stitch with Slip-stitch Edge.

Inc row Sl 1, knit front & back (kf&b), k to last 2 sts, kf&b, k1.

Repeat Inc row every 6th row 12 (10) or 11 (10, 9) or 15 (14, 13) times more—62 or 60 or 76 sts.

Adult's S–M, Bulky weight: 7 skeins FIESTA La Boheme in LB 1244 Rusty, 2 skeins La Luz in LL09 Lolite

• *one 13mm/½" (Child's)*
• *one 25mm/1" (Adult's)*

I used

• *3.5mm/US4*
• *4.5mm/US7*
• *5.5mm/US9*

• *3.25mm/D*
• *4mm/G*
• *5mm/H*

Child's 4: KOIGU Painter's Palette Premium Merino 2 skeins each in 133, 143, and 145; 1 skein in 1003

Work even until Sleeve measures 10 (12)" or 14", end with a WS row.
SHORTEN OR LENGTHEN HERE
Bind off loosely.
After Right Sleeve, do Finishing Step 9.
Repeat after Left Sleeve.

FINISHING
Attach all strips as follows:
• with crochet hook and contrasting yarn;
• with RS facing;
• beginning at cast-on edges unless directed otherwise;
• single crochet (see page 44) loosely through inside edges of slip sts (up lengths) OR through inside edges of bound-off sts (across shoulders or Sleeves).

Assemble 12 body strips

1 Attach Strip 1 to Strip 2.

2 Attach Strip 3 to Strip 2, forming a 3-strip rectangle.
Make 3 more rectangles with Strips 4–6, 7–9, and 10–12.

3 **Attach center-Back strip**
Attach one rectangle to side of Strip 13.
Attach second rectangle to other side of Strip 13.

4 **Attach Right-Front strip**
Attach third rectangle to Strip 14.

5 **Attach Left-Front strip**
Attach fourth rectangle to Strip 15.

6 **Make collar**
With main yarn, graft live sts of Strip 14 to live sts of Strip 15 at center Back neck (see page 46).

7 **Attach Fronts to Back**
Beginning at right shoulder, join Right Front to Right Back, making sure all crocheted lines match up.
Stop at beginning of center-Back strip, count number of bound-off sts at top of center-Back strip and slip sts of collar (side of Strips 14 and 15).
You will have more slip sts than bound-off sts.
Join as usual, space extra slip sts, and end at center Back.

8 Beginning at left shoulder, join Left Front to Left Back in same manner.

Adult´s S–M, Bulky weight (left): 7 skeins FIESTA La Boheme in LB 1074 Aster, 2 skeins La Luz in LL09 Lolite

Attach Sleeves

9

Begin at center of Right Sleeve and right shoulder seam.

Join one half of Sleeve top to garment side.

Return to center, turn work, and join other half of Sleeve to garment.

Repeat for Left Sleeve.

Edging

Begin at lower edge of Right Sleeve and work 1 sc in each cast-on stitch of cuff.

Work 3 sc at corner.

Make Sleeve seam by sc up Sleeve.

Continue to work sc around entire Front edge as follows:

- 1 sc in each sl st;
- 3 sc at every corner;
- 1 sc in every cast-on st.

Begin at lower edge of Left Sleeve and work in same way around Left Sleeve cuff then up Left Sleeve and around entire Back edge. End at underarm of Right Sleeve.

Work in tails.

Attach button to WS of Left Front, matching buttonhole.

Block, and steam press edging at corners.

Adult's S–M, Bulky weight (page 16):
MANOS DEL URUGUAY 100% Wool
6 skeins in 104 (A), 3 skeins in 112 (B), 1 skein in M

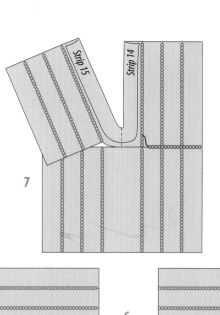

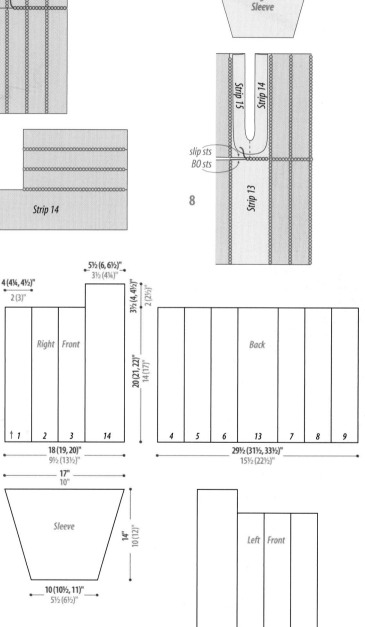

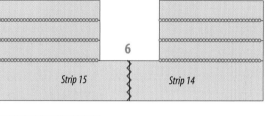

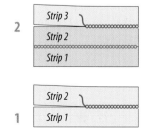

EXPERIence
- *intermediate*
- *stitch pattern through shaping*
- *reverse shaping*

OVERSIZED FIT

Child's 6–8 (10–12, Woman's S, M, L, 1X, 2X)

A 38 (43½, 45, 48½, 51½, 54, 59½)"

B (at sides) 16 (17½, 22, 23, 24, 25, 26)"

C 20 (23, 28½, 29, 29½, 30, 30½)"

Child's, Woman's
10cm/4"

20, 24
12, 13
- *multiple yarn*
- *single yarn*
- **over garter stitch or Purl Dash, garter stitch will get higher row gauge**
- *after blocking*

You'll need

3 X **2** OR **5**
- *Fine weight*
- *3 yarns held together*
- *550 (610) yds of each*
  OR
- *Bulky weight*
- *1080 (1200, 1320, 1450, 1620) yds*
- *wool or wool blend*

I used

- *6mm/US10*

- *5.5mm/I*

- *Five 25mm/1"*

BLANKET JACKET

I call this garment the 'blanket' jacket because it reminds me of one I sewed, as a teenager, out of a car blanket. This jacket has the same fringe as that original, plus it has the same warm, cozy, wrap-yourself-in-it feeling.

The woman's yarn is a short-color-change variegated, and the child's yarns are solids + a variegated. All are used in stitch patterns that blend colors.

I show 2 gauges: 13 sts and bulky yarn for the woman's, 12 sts and 3 fine yarns held together for the child's. If you use a bulky yarn for the child's, you may get an A measurement 2½–3" smaller. The jacket will still fit because the garment is shaped generously and the slightly finer gauge will not be as bulky.

You have other choices:
- *garter stitch or knit-and-purl pattern,*
- *round neck or shawl collar.*

I recommend garter stitch for the shawl collar because it is easier to manage through all the shaping and garter stitch is reversible.

You might notice that the C measurement does not match the schematics. This is because the jacket will stretch 2" wider across the shoulders with wearing (especially in the bulky yarn).

Purl Dash (multiple of 4 sts)
Row 1 (RS) K2, *k2, p2; repeat from* to last 2 sts, k2.
Rows 2, 4 K2, purl to last 2 sts, k2.
Row 3 K2, *p2, k2; repeat from* to last 2 sts, k2.
Repeat Rows 1–4.

Woman's M: 9 skeins MOUNTAIN COLORS New 3-ply Wool in Indian Corn
Child's 6–8: 2 balls each LION BRAND Wool-ease Sportweight in 153, 196, and 099 (held together)

Notes

1 See *Skills-at-a-glance,* page 228, for e-wrap cast-on, slip stitch, SSK, k2tog, kf&b, eyelet buttonholes, and attaching fringe. *2* Heavy lines on schematic indicate slip-st edges. *3* When only 2 numbers are offered, the first is for the Child's sizes, the second is for the Woman's sizes. *4* Use e-wrap cast-on throughout.

BACK

Shape lower edge

Cast on 6 sts.

Garter stitch: *Row 1* (RS) Knit.

Row 2 Cast on 2 sts, knit to end.

Repeat last row.

Purl Dash: *Row 1* (RS) Knit.

Row 2 Cast on 2 sts, k2, purl to last 2 sts, k2.

Row 3 Cast on 2 sts, k2, *k2, p2; repeat from* to last 2 sts, k2.

Row 4 Cast on 2 sts, k2, purl to last 2 sts, k2.

Repeat last 2 rows.

Both stitch pats Continue casting on 2 sts at the beginning of every row to 56 (64, 72, 76, 80, 88, 96) sts.

  If working Purl Dash, next RS row will be Row 3.

Body

Work even until piece measures 8 (9, 11½, 12, 12½, 13, 13½)" at sides. End with a WS row.

SHORTEN OR LENGTHEN HERE

Shape armhole

Bind off 2 (2, 3, 4, 5, 6, 7) sts at beginning of next 2 rows.

Dec row (RS) K1, SSK, work to last 3 sts, k2tog, k1.

Repeat Dec row every RS row 4 (8, 3, 4, 5, 8, 11) times more—42 (58) sts.

Work even until armhole measures 7 (7½, 8½, 9, 9½, 10, 10½)". End with a WS row.

Shape shoulders and neck

Adult sizes only Bind off 3 sts at beginning of next 6 rows.

Right shoulder, all sizes Bind off 3 sts at beginning of next RS row, work to 10 (8) sts on right needle. Turn.

*Bind off 1 st at neck edge 2 times. AT SAME TIME, bind off 4 (3) sts at armhole edge 2 times.

Bind off center 16 (18) sts, then work to end of row.

Left shoulder Bind off 3 sts at beginning of next row.

Work as Right shoulder from* to end.

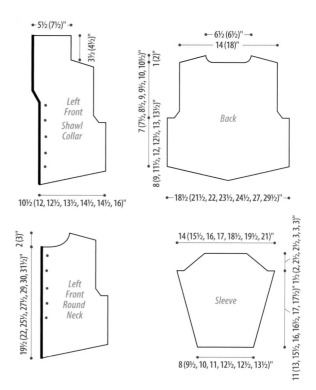

LEFT FRONT
Shape lower edge
Cast on 4 sts.

Garter stitch: *Row 1* (RS) Knit.

Row 2 With yarn in front, sl 1 purlwise (sl-st edge), knit to end.

Row 3 Cast on 2 sts, knit to end.

Repeat last 2 rows.

Purl Dash: *Row 1* (RS) Knit.

Row 2 Knit.

Row 3 Cast on 2 sts, k6.

Row 4, 6 (WS) K2, purl to last 2 sts, k2.

Row 5 Cast on 2 sts, k2, *k2, p2; repeat from* to last 2 sts, k2.

Repeat last 2 rows.

Both stitch pats Continue casting on 2 sts at the beginning of every RS row to 32 (36, 40, 44, 48, 48, 52) sts.

  If working Garter stitch, continue sl-st edge.

  If working Purl Dash, next RS row will be Row 3.

Body
Work even to same length as Back at sides, end with a WS row.

  Choices for neck shapings are introduced here. Continue stitch pat through all shaping.

Shape armhole for round neck
Bind off 2 (2, 2, 4, 5, 6, 7) sts at beginning of next RS row.

Dec row (RS) K1, SSK, work to end.

Repeat Dec row every RS row 7 (11, 4, 6, 9, 8, 11) times more—22 (33) sts.

Work even until armhole measures 7 (7½, 8½, 9, 9½, 10, 10½)", end with a RS row.

Shape round neck

At beginning of WS rows, bind off 5 (9) sts once, 2 (2) sts once, and 1 st 4 times—11 (18) sts.

Work even until armhole measures same length as Back, end with a WS row.

Go to Shape shoulder, all versions.

Shape armhole for shawl collar

Bind off 2 (2, 3, 4, 5, 6, 7) sts at beginning of next RS row.

Dec row (RS) K1, SSK, work to end.

Repeat Dec row once more—28 (32, 36, 38, 41, 40, 43) sts.

Begin shawl collar shaping: *Next RS row* K1, SSK (armhole dec), work to last 2 sts, kf&b (shawl collar inc), k1.

Don't forget sl-st edge.

Work shawl collar incs every 4 rows 4 (9) times more, AT SAME TIME, work armhole decs every RS row 5 (9, 2, 4, 7, 6, 9) times more—27 (43) sts.

Work even until armhole measures same length as Back, end with a WS row.

Shape shoulder, all versions

Adult sizes only Bind off 3 sts at armhole edge 3 times.

All sizes Bind off at armhole edge 3 sts once, and 4 (3) sts twice—0 sts for round neck, 16 (25) sts for shawl collar.

Finish shawl collar

Work collar sts even for 3½ (4½)", end with a WS row. Put sts on holder.

All sizes Mark points on Left Front for 5 buttons, beginning 1" below round neck shaping or immediately below start of shawl collar and ending 6" from lowest point.

RIGHT FRONT
Shaped lower edge
Cast on 4 sts.
Garter stitch: *Row 1* (RS) Knit.
Row 2 Cast on 2 sts, knit to end.
Row 3 With yarn in front, sl 1 purlwise (for sl-st edge), knit to end.
Repeat last 2 rows.
Purl Dash stitch: *Row 1* (RS) Knit.
Row 2 Cast on 2 sts, k2, p2, k2.
Row 3 K2, p2, k2.
Row 4, 6 Cast on 2 sts, k2, purl to last 2 sts, k2.
Row 5 K2, *k2, p2; repeat from* to last 2 sts, k2.
Row 7 K2, *p2, k2; repeat from* to last 2 sts, k2.
Repeat last 4 rows.
Both stitch pats Continue in this manner, casting on 2 sts at the beginning of every WS row, to 32 (36, 40, 44, 48, 48, 52) sts.
Body
Work even to same length as Back at side, AT SAME TIME
Make eyelet buttonholes On RS rows that correspond to button markers, work 3 sts, k2tog, yo, work to end.
Round neck, shawl collar, shoulder shaping
Work as Left Front, but reverse shaping as follows:
- work armhole bind-off at beginning of WS row;
- work armhole decreases in last 3 sts as k2tog, k1;
- for round neck shaping, bind-off at beginning of RS rows;
- work shawl collar increases in 2nd st of RS rows;
- bind off shoulders at beginning of WS rows;
- work collar to 1 row short of left collar, end with RS row.

SLEEVES
Cast on 24 (28, 32, 36, 40, 40, 44) sts.
Work Garter or Purl Dash for 2".
Inc row (RS) K1, kf&b, work to last 2 sts, kf&b, k1.
Repeat Inc row every 4 (4, 6, 6, 6, 4, 4) rows 8 (8, 9, 9, 9, 11, 11) times more—42 (46, 52, 56, 60, 64, 68) sts.
Work even until Sleeve measures 11 (13, 15½, 16, 16½, 17, 17½)", end with a WS row.
SHORTEN OR LENGTHEN HERE
Shape sleeve cap
Bind off 2 (2, 3, 4, 5, 6, 7) sts at beginning of next 2 rows—38 (42, 46, 48, 50, 52, 54) sts.

Bind off 2 sts at beginning of next 2 rows 3 (4, 5, 5, 6, 6, 6) times—26 (26, 26, 28, 26, 28, 30) sts. Bind off 4 (4, 2, 3, 2, 3, 4) sts at beginning of next 2 rows. Bind off remaining 18 (22) sts.

FINISHING
Sew shoulder seams.
For shawl collar Graft sts together at center back (page 46). Sew collar to back neck, easing to fit.
For round neck If edge needs to be neatened, work slip st crochet around curved neck edges (page 44).
Sew side seams.
Sew Sleeves into armholes.
Sew Sleeve seams.
Try garment on, then sew buttons to Left Front to match buttonholes and with desired overlap.
Attach fringe
Cut 8 (10)" lengths for body and 6 (8)" lengths for sleeves. Attach 2 strands at every cast-on step of lower edges and every second stitch of cuffs, working tails into fringe. Trim fringe.

Man's L: 11 skeins MOUNTAIN COLORS New
3-ply Wool in Marias Falls
Child's 6–8: 3 balls each PATONS Kroy in 54108
and 54561, 2 balls BERNAT So Soft in 76760

EXPERience

- *intermediate*
- *stitch pattern through shaping*

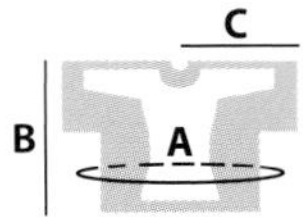

OVERSIZED FIT

Child's 6-8 (10-12)
Man's S (M, L, 1X, 2X)

A 36 (38½, 47, 50½, 52, 57, 60½)"

B 17 (19½, 27, 27½, 28, 28½, 29)"

C 21½ (24, 32½, 33½, 34½, 35½, 36½)"

10cm/4"

22

12, 13

- *multiple yarn*
- *single yarn*
- **using larger needles**
- **over Broken Rib**
- **after blocking**

You'll need

- **Medium + 2 Super fine yarns held together**
  - **575 (612) yds each**
  - *Bulky weight*
- **1210 (1350, 1480, 1620, 1750) yds**
- *wool or wool blend(s)*

I used

- **5mm/US8 and 6mm/US10**

- **5mm/H**

- *Four (six) 25mm/1"*

JEREMY'S JACKET

Having made the Blanket Jacket for the women and kids, I wanted to do something for the guys. I thought about my son, Jeremy, who is always cold. (This is no statement about Canada: he is just a skinny young man who prefers hot climates.) I looked at the colors available in this yarn that I love, and—there it was—Missouri River Blues. Perfect! My son is a blues musician, and his dad was a Missouri boy. (PS The name of the color has been changed to Marias Falls.)

I show 2 gauges: 13 sts and bulky yarn for the man's, 12 sts and 1 medium + 2 superfine weights together for the child's. If you use a bulky yarn for the child's, you may get an A measurement 2½–3" smaller. The jacket will likely still fit because the garment is shaped generously and the slightly finer gauge will not be as bulky.

The man's yarn is a short-color-change variegated, and the child's yarns are various variegateds (see page 40). All are used in a stitch pattern that blends colors.

The C measurement does not match the schematic because the garment may stretch 2" wider across the shoulders with wearing (especially in the single yarn).

Broken Rib (multiple of 4 sts + 2)
RS rows *K2, p2; repeat from* to last 2 sts, k2.
WS rows Purl.

Notes
1 See *Skills-at-a-glance*, page 228, for k2tog, SSK, slip stitch, lifted increase, and eyelet buttonholes. **2** When only 2 numbers are given, the first is for Child's sizes, the second is for Man's. **3** Heavy lines on schematic indicate slip-st edge. **4** Maintain stitch pattern through all shaping.

BACK
With smaller needles, cast on 54 (58, 78, 82, 86, 94, 98) sts.
Work 6 rows Broken Rib.

10 (11)"
•15½ (16½, 18, 19, 20½, 21½, 22½)•

Sleeve

11½ (13½, 18½, 19½, 19½, 20, 20½, 19½)"
2 (3, 3, 3½, 3½, 3½, 3½)"

7½ (8½, 10½, 11½, 13, 13, 14)"

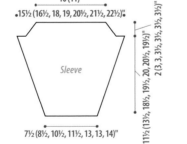

3½ (4, 6½, 6, 6½, 6½, 7¼)"
6½ (6½)"
1 (2)"
1 (2)"

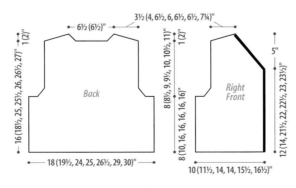

Back

Right Front

16 (18½, 25, 25½, 26, 26½, 27)"

8 (8½, 9, 9½, 10, 10½, 11)"
8 (10, 16, 16, 16, 16)"

5"

12 (14, 21½, 22, 22½, 23, 23½)"

18 (19½, 24, 25, 26½, 29, 30)"
10 (11½, 14, 14, 15½, 16½)"

Change to larger needles, and work until piece measures 8 (10, 16, 16, 16, 16, 16)", end with a WS row.
SHORTEN OR LENGTHEN HERE

Shape armhole
Bind off 2 (2, 3, 4, 6, 8, 10) sts at beginning of next 2 rows—50 (54, 72, 74, 74, 78, 78) sts.
Dec row (RS) K2, SSK, work Broken Rib to last 4 sts, k2tog, k2.
Repeat Dec row every RS row 4 times more—40 (44, 62, 64, 64, 68, 68) sts remain.
Work even until armhole measures 8 (8½, 9, 9½, 10, 10½, 11)", end with a WS row.

Shape shoulders and back neck
Bind off 0 (4) sts at beginning of next 0 (4) rows.
Right shoulder Bind off 3 (4) sts at beginning of next RS row, then work until there are 9 (11, 10, 11, 11, 13, 13) sts on right needle. Turn.
*Bind off 1 st at neck edge 2 times, AT SAME TIME bind off 3 (4) sts at armhole edge once, and 4 (6, 4, 5, 5, 7, 7) sts once.
Left shoulder Bind off center 16 (18) sts, then work to end of row. Bind off 3 (4) sts at beginning of next WS row. Work as Right shoulder from* to end.

RIGHT FRONT
With smaller needles, cast on 30 (34, 42, 46, 46, 50, 54) sts.
Work 6 rows Broken Rib EXCEPT on all WS rows slip last (center front) stitch p-wise.
Change to larger needles, and work to same length as Back to underarm, end with a RS row.

Shape armhole
Bind off 2 (3, 3, 4, 6, 8, 10) sts at beginning of next WS row.
Dec row (RS) K2, work Broken Rib to last 4 sts, k2tog, k2.
Repeat Dec row every RS row 4 times more—23 (26, 34, 37, 35, 37, 39) sts.
Work even until armhole measures 4 (4½, 5½, 6, 6½, 7, 7½, 8)", end with a WS row.

Shape V-neck
Dec row (RS) K1, SSK, work to end.
Child's version Repeat Dec row every RS row 12 (13) times more—10 (12) sts.
Man's version Repeat Dec row 2 out of every 3 RS rows 12 (15, 13, 15, 15) times more—21 (21, 21, 21, 23) sts.
All versions Work even until armhole measures same length as Back to shoulder, end with a RS row.

Shape shoulder
At beginning of WS rows, bind off 0 (4) sts 0 (2) times, then 3 (4) sts twice.
Bind off remaining 4 (6, 5, 5, 5, 5, 7) sts.
Mark for 4 (6) buttons, with first marker 1" below first neck decrease, last 1" above lower edge, and others spaced evenly between.

LEFT FRONT
Work as for Right Front EXCEPT on WS rows, slip first st p-wise; AT SAME TIME on RS rows that correspond to button markers, work eyelet buttonhole in last 5 sts: SSK, yo, p1, k2; AND reverse shaping at armhole (k2, SSK) and V-neck (k2tog, k1) on RS rows.

SLEEVES
With smaller needles, cast on 22 (26, 34, 38, 42, 42, 46) sts.
Work 6 rows Broken Rib.
Change to larger needles.
Inc row (RS) K2, work lifted inc in next st (inc 1), work in pattern to last 3 sts, inc 1, k2.
Repeat Inc row every 4th (6th) row 11 (11, 11, 11, 11, 13, 13) times more—46 (50, 58, 62, 66, 70, 74) sts.
Work even until Sleeve measures 11½ (13½, 18½, 19½, 20, 20½, 19½)", end with a WS row.
SHORTEN OR LENGTHEN HERE

Shape sleeve cap
Bind off 2 (2, 3, 4, 6, 8, 10) sts at beginning of next 2 rows.
Dec row (RS) K2, SSK, work to last 4 sts, k2tog, k2.
Repeat Dec row 5 (7, 7, 8, 8, 8, 8) times more—30 (36) sts.
Bind off at beginning of next 2 rows 2 sts once, then 4 sts once.
Bind off remaining sts.

FINISHING
Sew shoulder seams.
If back neck needs to be neatened, work slip st crochet around curved neck edges (page 44).
Sew side seams.
Sew Sleeves into armholes.
Sew Sleeve seams.
Try garment on, and sew buttons to Left Front to match buttonholes and with desired overlap.

CHOKER CUFF

This piece was designed as a minimal scarf—to be worn in warmer months and climes. But then the model wore it as a cuff, and we all loved it! Maybe it was always meant to be a cuff? Certainly, it was meant to be worn both ways.

The yarn used is a short-color-change variegated (see page 40).

Note
See *Skills-at-a-glance,* page 228, for eyelet buttonhole.

CUFF
Cast on 12 sts.
Knit all stitches, all rows, until piece fits comfortably around neck, stretching slightly.
Knit 2½" more.
Make eyelet buttonhole, Next row
K4, yo, k2tog, knit to end.
Knit 2" more.
Bind off.
Sew in tails.
To wear, thread cast-on end through buttonhole.

Approx 3"

0

Approx 18"

↑ *Direction of knitting*

1 skein GREAT ADIRONDACK Tribbles in Serengeti.

Experience
• *beginner's first project*
  • *no shaping*
  • *no finishing*

One size fits all

10cm/4"

14–15
14–15

• *over garter stitches and ridges (knit every row)*

You'll need

1 2 3 4 **5** 6

• *Bulky weight*
  • *26 yds*
  • *novelty yarn*

I used

• *5.5–6mm/US9–10*

EXPErience

- *easy-intermediate*
- *repetitive stitch pattern*
- *minimal shaping*
- *minimal finishing*

STANDARD FIT

S (M, L, 1X)
A 25½ (27½, 31, 34½)"
B 17½ (18, 18½, 19)"
C 51½ (55, 62, 68½)"

10cm/4"

26 🔲 14

- *over stitch pattern*
- *after blocking*

You'll need

1 2 3 **4** 5 6

- *Medium weight*
- *380 (420, 500, 560) yds*
- *wool or wool with nylon*

I used

- *5.5mm/US9, 60cm/24"*
- *for length, not to work in the round*

&

- *1 yd elastic cord for waistband*

Skirt M: 4 skeins MANOS DEL URUGUAY 100% Wool in 110
Pullover M: 9 skeins CLASSIC ELITE Renaissance in 7150 (pattern on page 56)

NANCY'S SKIRT

Remember the Knit-round scarf in *The Knit Stitch,* worn as a skirt? Then there was a Not-knit-round scarf in *The Purl Stitch,* also modeled as a skirt. I loved the look of the skirt, but it didn't quite fit my girth. Sooooo, here's a version actually intended and shaped to be a skirt, named for my sister, who test knit it.

Since it's made of a wonderful variegated yarn, it fits in this 'Let-the-yarn-do-the-work' chapter. But it could be made from anything as long as it's wool. Why wool? Because wool will not 'seat.' And if it does? The skirt has no front or back shaping, so just turn it around.

2×2 Rib (multiple of 4 sts+2)
RS rows K2, *p2, k2; repeat from* to end.
WS rows P2, *k2, p2; repeat from* to end.

A Rib-with-lace (multiple of 4 sts+2)
RS rows K2, *yo, p2tog, k2; repeat from* to end.
WS rows P2, *yo, p2tog, p2; repeat from* to end.

B Rib-with-lace (multiple of 10 sts+2)
RS rows K2, *yo, p2tog, k4, yo, p2tog, k2; repeat from* to end.
WS rows P2, *yo, p2tog, p4, yo, p2tog, p2; repeat from* to end.

C Rib-with-lace (multiple of 6 sts + 2)
RS rows *K4, yo, p2tog; repeat from* to last 2 sts, k2.
WS rows P2, *yo, p2tog, p4; repeat from* to end.

Note
See *Skills-at-a-glance*, page 228, for k2tog, p2tog, SSK, and yarn over (yo).

SKIRT
Cast on 182 (194, 218, 242) sts.
Work 2×2 Rib for 1", end with a WS row.
Work A Rib-with-lace to 7½ (8, 8½, 9)", end with a WS row.
SHORTEN OR LENGTHEN HERE
First dec row *K2, yo, p2tog, k1, SSK, k2tog, k1, yo, p2tog;
repeat from* to last 2 sts, k2—152 (162, 182, 202) sts.
Begin with WS row, work B Rib-with-lace until Skirt
measures 11½ (12, 12½, 13)", end with a WS row.
Second dec row *K2, yo, p2tog, SSK, k2tog, yo, p2tog;
repeat from* to last 2 sts, k2—122 (130, 146, 162) sts.
Begin with WS row, work A Rib-with-lace until Skirt
measures 14½ (15, 15½, 16)", end with WS row.
Third dec row *K1, SSK, k2tog, k1, yo, p2tog; repeat
from* to last 2 sts, k2—92 (98, 110, 122) sts.
Begin with WS row, work C Rib-with-lace until Skirt
measures 16½ (17, 17½, 18)", end with a WS row.
Work St st (k on RS, p on WS) until Skirt measures 18
(18½, 19, 19½)".
Bind off very loosely, leaving long tail to secure waistband.

FINISHING
Seam, taking 1 stitch from each side into seam allowance.
Wash and block to shape.
Fold top ½" to RS, then sew down. Run elastic cord
through waistband. Knot cord, and bury tails.

M: 4 skeins MANOS DEL URUGUAY 100% Wool in 100

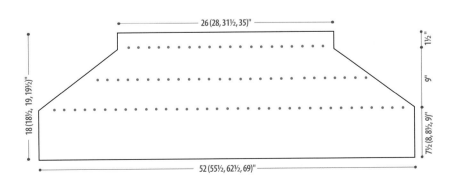

Variegated yarns

Variegated yarn refers to multi-colored yarn. They are very beautiful and very seductive. We buy them and then wonder what to do with them. How to make best use of such gorgeous and precious material?

If you've knit something in a variegated yarn and are not happy with the result, you might be able to overdye it. See Oops, page 224, and check out other rescue possibilities for common color mistakes.

It would take a great deal of swatching and math to figure out exactly how stacking will occur and how it will change in pieces of different widths. And it would then change again as the piece is shaped. If you wish to maintain how the color repeats, work unshaped pieces of the same width (like the strips of the Faith jacket, page 24), or work in the round.

SHORT, MEDIUM, LONG SPACE OF COLOR
Shown here are what I see as 3 categories of variegated yarns:
• short space of color, in which the color changes quickly—in 4" or less,
• medium space of color, in which the color changes less quickly—anywhere from 4–24",
• long space of color, in which the color changes very slowly—in 24" or more.

Short color change
The short change generally doesn't give much trouble, although you might prefer it in something other than stockinette stitch. The garments of this chapter explore a range of stitch patterns other than stockinette stitch.

Medium color change
The medium change can give blotches of color, depending upon how the colors stack (line up) on subsequent rows. The width of the piece determines how this stacking will occur, and the stacking will change with different widths.

It's fun to just knit and let a medium change 'do it's thing.' But if you wish to minimize stacking, try using 2 balls (working 2 rows from one then 2 rows from the other) or try using 3 balls (working 1 row from each, see page 42).

Here's an example of short color change...

...and medium color change...

...and long color change.

Short-color-change yarn in garter and stockinette stitch.

Shows stacking (in diagonal yellow line) of medium-color-change yarn in garter and stockinette stitch.

Long color change

The long change produces stripes, and this is a problem when the pieces are different widths. For example, the 12" circumference legwarmers show stripes 2" tall: these could be the sleeves of a garment. So, if the body were knit in-the-round to 48", the stripes would be only half an inch tall. Or if the front of the garment were knit flat and 24" across, the stripes would be only 1" tall. And if the piece was shaped (at the armhole), the stripes would change again.

This uneven striping is not an effect we want. But we can deal with it by working patterns whose pieces are similar width.

Maximum Legwarmers (shown here in Noro Kureyon) and the Einstein Coat (shown here in Noro Iro) are both patterns from *The Knit Stitch* and both have pieces close enough to the same width that the striping is fairly uniform.

Einstein Coat

Maximum Legwarmers

We can sometimes blur the striping of variegated yarns by working in a stitch pattern that blends the color by interrupting the color sequence. We can do this very simply by moving the color from the previous row up to the current row—by purling a right-side stitch, by knitting a wrong-side stitch, by slipping a stitch.

If you consider the photos on these 2 pages and on the next page, you'll see this happening in garter stitch. It can also happen in reverse stockinette. And if you look through the patterns of this chapter, you'll find other stitch patterns that also do this work.

Working 1-row-of-each is easy enough except that it can become terribly tangled. To manage this, lay balls in sequence and move them each time. (If they unravel easily, put them each in their own little baggie.)

You could make this fabric with 5 yarns. The trick is that it needs to be an odd number. But more than 5 gets difficult to manage.

When working a fabric of 1-row-in-each, you can put the knitting down, come back to it, then wonder which end of a circular needle and which yarn you should be working with next. Here's the trick: the edge with 2 yarns hanging is where you should start working, and the yarn hanging furthest down is the one you should introduce next.

MAKING YOUR OWN VARIEGATED
1-row-in-each
It's fun to take 3 yarns and work 1 row of each to produce your own variegated yarn. The effect is wonderful if some or all of the yarns are variegated, but you might also like the look of solids.

To see if you are going to like a 1-row-of-each combination, take all 3 and wrap them in sequence around a piece of cardboard. Look at them at close range but also at a distance.

1-row-in-each, in garter and stockinette.

1-row-in-each, in garter and stockinette.

More than one yarn at a time
You can also produce your own 'variegated' yarn by using several yarns as 1. To see if you are going to like the combination, wrap them together around a piece of cardboard. Look at it at close range but also at a distance.

2 yarns together, in garter and stockinette.

Yarn combinations

Of course, when we combine more than 1 yarn, we get a thicker fabric. Here's my experience of what the various combinations can produce.
- 2 superfine = 1 light
- 3 superfine = 1 medium
- 1 superfine + 1 light = 1 medium
- 2 fine = 1 medium
- 3 fine = 1 bulky
- 2 superfine + 1 light = 1 bulky
- 2 light = bulky
- 1 medium + 1 fine = bulky

Re-gauging a pattern

Sometimes the perfect color appears but not in a yarn that will work to the gauge of the pattern. What to do? If it's close, you can follow these steps to get what you want.
- Do a gauge swatch in the new yarn; count the stitches in 4", then divide by 4 to determine the number of stitches in 1". (Let's say there are 20 stitches in 4"; 20 stitches ÷ 4" = 5 stitches in 1".)
- Look at the pattern as it exists, choose your size, then look at the schematic to see what width the front or back is. (Let's say the size you want is 22" wide.)
- Multiply this width by your gauge over 1". (22" × 5 stitches/inch = 110 stitches.)
- Look at the pattern again. Is there a size that has close to 110 stitches in it? (It might be a smaller size than you want, or a larger size. This doesn't matter. All it has to have is 110 stitches.)
- If there is a size that gives the number of stitches you need, follow the pattern for this size by using the number of stitches for this size but knitting to the length you want.

If one size has too few stitches and the next size has too many, can you figure out how to work between the sizes? (For example, you need 110 stitches. Maybe the S offers 104 and the M offers 114. Can you see that you could work between these 2 sets of directions?) Don't forget to consider pattern multiples and if you need an even/odd number of stitches.

Of course, there are situations where none of the above apply: perhaps there is NOT a size that offers anything close to the number of stitches you need. Then you have the option of re-calculating everything, and here's an easy way to do that.
- Do a gauge swatch in the new yarn; count the stitches in 4". (Let's say there are 20 stitches in 4".)
- Look at the pattern's gauge over 4". (Let's say there are 22 stitches in 4".)
- Divide your gauge by the pattern's gauge. (20 ÷ 22 = .91)
- You can now take all the numbers of the pattern and multiply by .91 to get the number of stitches for your size. Sometimes you'll have to round up or down, but you can do it!
- Don't forget to consider pattern multiples and if you need an even/odd number of stitches.
- Again, knit the number of stitches you calculate but to the length you want.

Obviously there are more options to produce thicker yarns than thinner. The options are practically unlimited to produce a super bulky yarn, so go ahead and try just about anything. To find out what works, don't forget the twist-'em-against-each-other test. (See page 134 of *The Knit Stitch* or page 155 of *The Purl Stitch*.)

Other combinations are possible. You can, for example, produce a bulky fabric with 2 medium yarns. But it will be very heavy. At some point, even if you get gauge with whatever combination you have used, you need to examine the wearability of the fabric.

To get an appropriate gauge, I generally find that I have to use larger needles on these combinations than I would on a single yarn. The reason for this is that the multiple yarns tend to sit behind each other; the larger needles spread them out to gauge.

I show this work done in a contrast color (green) because it is easier for you to see.

Single crochet to join or embellish

Sometimes an easy and effective alternative to a knit edging is to finish a piece of knitting with a row of single crochet. The result—whether a seam or an edging—is pretty and flexible.

1 Holding knitting and yarn in left hand and crochet hook in right, insert crochet hook under 2 threads.

2 Take hook under yarn,...

3 ...then draw yarn through knitting (1 loop on hook).

I demonstrate this work done under 2 threads of a garter stitch edge and to embellish. But the 3 other situations in which you might use it are shown in the 'set-up' photos below. Use these to replace Step 1 (above), then proceed as directed.

 **OR**  **OR**

Under 2 garter threads, to seam.

Under 2 slip stitch threads, to embellish.

Under 2 inside slip stitch threads, to seam.

I find this technique a little too tight for a seam.

Slip stitch crochet to embellish

Sometimes we just want to tighten or neaten an edge with a row of slip stitch crochet.

1 Holding knitting and yarn in left hand and crochet hook in right, insert crochet hook under 2 threads.

2 Take hook under yarn,...

3 ...then draw yarn through knitting (1 loop on hook).

4 Insert crochet hook under next 2 threads.

SINGLE CROCHET • SLIP STITCH

4 Take hook over knitting, to left of yarn,…

5 …then under yarn;…

6 …now draw yarn through loop on hook (1 loop on hook).

7 Insert crochet hook under next 2 threads of knitting.

8 Take hook to left of yarn and then under yarn,…

9 …then draw yarn through knitting (2 loops now on hook).

10 Take hook over knitting and under yarn again, and draw yarn through both loops on hook (1 loop now on hook/1 single crochet made).

Repeat Steps 7–10 to end. To finish, cut yarn and draw through loop on hook.

5 Take hook to left of yarn…

6 …and then under yarn,

7 …then draw yarn through knitting and through loop on hook (1 loop on hook/1 slip stitch made).

Repeat Steps 4–7 to end. To finish, cut yarn and draw through loop on hook.

Grafting in garter stitch

You will set this up with one piece ending with a wrong-side row (with the bumps close to the needle) and one ending with a right-side row (with the bumps not so close to the needle).

Even if you know how to graft the toes of socks, which is usually done in stockinette stitch, it's another useful skill to know how to graft in this other common stitch pattern. Where I most often find myself doing this is in shawl collars, often done in garter (which is reversible). So, grafting is nice, because then the seam is invisible and the collar can be worn both up or down.

It doesn't matter if RS or WS is facing; what's important is where the bumps are.

Have both pieces on needles; if straights, have the points of both needles in the same place.
Hold so needle with close bumps is the lower needle, needle with not-so-close bumps is the upper needle.

Here's what you need to know to work through what follows.
- Knitwise means insert the tapestry needle as if it were a knitting needle and you were preparing to knit.
- Purlwise means insert the tapestry needle as if it were a knitting needle and you were preparing to purl.
- Once a stitch is removed from the knitting needle, it is not touched again.
- Do not pull too tightly as you are working; you will adjust tension later.
- Be careful not to split stitches or yarn as you work.
- In the directions below, 'needle' refers to a knitting needle (not the tapestry needle).

If your pieces begin with slip stitches, work as follows.

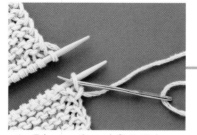

1 Take yarn through first stitch on lower needle purlwise; leave stitch on needle.

2 Take yarn through first stitch on upper needle purlwise; remove stitch from needle.

3 Take yarn through first stitch on lower needle knitwise; remove stitch from needle.
Now proceed with the steps for grafting in garter that follow.

GRAFTING GARTER STITCH

To graft garter stitch

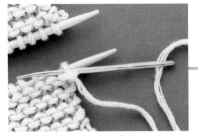

1 Take yarn through first stitch on lower needle purlwise; leave stitch on needle.

2 Take yarn through first stitch on upper needle knitwise; remove stitch from needle.

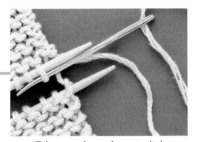

3 Take yarn through next stitch on upper needle purlwise; leave stitch on needle.

4 Take yarn through first stitch on lower needle knitwise; remove stitch from needle.

5 Take yarn through next stitch on lower needle purlwise; leave stitch on needle.

Repeat Steps 2–5 until 1 stitch remains on each needle, ending with Step 5.
Repeat Step 2.
Repeat Step 4.
Starting at beginning of row, tighten grafting to appropriate tension.

Once you get going with this, it might help to just think 'knit, purl, knit, purl.'

I don't often graft in garter. Sometimes, even when the pieces are knit in garter, I will graft in stockinette stitch and then pull the grafting line tight (for a seam with no seam allowance). I do this when I want stability—when grafting is used for a seam that needs a little firmness (like at the back neck, where saddles meet).

And I'll graft in stockinette when the pieces to be joined were not set up for grafting in garter. For example, it would have taken some work, in Cynthia's Scarf, to know which edges of which squares were to join with which and then decide which should be stopped 1 row short to graft in garter.

I'll also join garter stitch pieces with a 3-needle bind-off for stability and a decorative detail, as done to join the squares of Cynthia's Afghan.

I will use grafting in garter when the pieces are knit in garter and when I know there will be no stress on the join—like in the shawl collar of the Faith Jacket of this chapter.

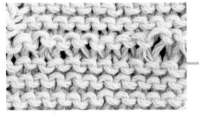

Here's the result before tightening.

Here is the final result.

EXPERience
- *easy intermediate*
- *simple shaping*
- *mid-level finishing*

STANDARD FIT

S (M, L, 1X, 2X)

A *35½ (40, 44½, 49½, 54)"*
B *19½ (20, 20½, 21, 21½)"*
C *29 (29½, 30, 30½, 31)"*

10cm/4"

30, 28

21, 19

- *over stockinette stitch*
- *using larger needles*
- *after blocking*

You'll need

 3 OR **4**

- *Light weight*

A • *285 (340, 400, 460, 525) yds*

B–E • *190 (230, 270, 310, 355) yds each*

- *Medium weight*

A • *270 (320, 375, 435, 475) yds*

B–E • *175 (210, 245, 285, 325) yds each*

I used

- *3.5mm/US4*
- *4mm/US6*

50cm/20" long

SKINNY STRIPES

Whether you choose the funnel or V-neck, here is a fun way to play with stripes. Note that you will be a little challenged as you keep track of rows and shaping, but the pattern guides you, and you'll learn a lot!

This shape reappears in this book: see Nancy's Skirt, page 38, and Not Mrs. D's Suit, page 144. So I'd like to say something about its styling…. Yes, it is 'boxy,' and I know there are those who don't appreciate boxy. But, in my experience, this is a very flattering style on most bodies. If you are wearing something that fits to your hips and waist, a boxy sweater sitting above makes everything below look slimmer. Most of us benefit from that!

The funnel neck uses a mix of tonal ranges:
- *main color/darkest color, navy (A);*
- *color close to complementary of main color, dark red-orange (B);*
- *light version of previous color, tint of red-orange (C);*
- *light version of main color, tone of blue (D);*
- *light version of color analogous to main color, tone of violet (E).*

The V-neck uses tones + neutrals:
- *main color/darkest color, dark tone of red-violet (A);*
- *pale version of color next to main color, red (E);*
- *analogous color to main color, red-orange (B);*
- *light neutral, oatmeal (C);*
- *dark neutral, taupe (D).*

Notes
1 See *Skills-at-a-glance*, page 228, for SSK, k2tog, SSP, p2tog, and lifted inc. *2* Work St st (knit on RS, purl on WS). *3* If you run out of something, just substitute with another color before buying another ball. *4* The funnel is knit to 19 sts, the V-neck to 21. When 2 sets of numbers are given, the green are for V-neck, the red are for funnel neck.

BACK
With any color but A, cast on 95 (107, 119, 133, 145) or 86 (98, 108, 120, 130) sts.
Work St st in 28-row stripe pattern as follows (each number indicates the number of rows in that color):

*2A, 1D, 1A, 1E, 1C, 1B, 1C, 1A, 2D, 1A, 2B, 1C, 1E, 2A, 1B, 1C, 2E, 1B, 2C, 1A, 1E, 1D; repeat from *.
  Carry all colors up the sides.
  Work on a circular needle without cutting yarn (see page 70).
  If you mess up the color repeat, don't worry about it. Just get right as soon as you can.
Work even until piece measures 10½".
SHORTEN OR LENGTHEN HERE
  Note where armhole bind-off occurs in color sequence.
Shape armhole
Bind off 3 (4, 6, 8, 10) sts at beginning of next 2 rows.
Dec row Work 1, SSK on RS (or p2tog on WS), work to last 3 sts, k2tog on RS (or SSP on WS), work 1.
  To maintain the color pattern, you might need to work the Dec row on a purl side.
Repeat Dec row every 2 rows 2 (7, 11, 16, 20) or 2 (7, 10, 14, 17) times more—83 or 74 sts.
Work even until armhole measures 7½ (8, 8½, 9, 9½)", end with a WS row.
Shape shoulders
Funnel neck only At beginning of row, bind off 3 sts 8 times, then 4 sts twice—42 sts.
  If you think you need a larger head opening, bind off fewer sts in the final shoulder bind off.
  If you want the funnel neck to not have a seam, put the neck sts onto a holder. Work the other piece. After sewing the shoulder seams, put all neck sts onto one circular needle and continue.
Continue over remaining sts, in color pattern, for 2–3".
Bind off all sts very loosely.
V-neck only Bind off 4 sts at beginning of next 2 rows.
Right shoulder Bind off 4 sts at beginning of next RS row, work to 17 sts on right needle. Turn. Put center 33 sts on holder.
*Bind off 1 st at neck edge twice AT SAME TIME at armhole edge, bind off 4 sts twice, then 7 sts once.
Left shoulder Return to 21 sts, RS facing.
Work 1 RS row.
Bind off 4 sts next WS row. Work as right shoulder from * to end.

FRONT
Funnel neck only Work as Back to end.
V-neck only Work as Back until armhole measures 1½ (2, 2½, 3, 3½)", end with a WS row.
Shape left V-neck
Work 41 sts (to center). Put center st on holder.

Work 1 row over left Front sts.

If needed for size, continue armhole shaping at same time as V-neck shaping.

Dec row Decrease in 3 sts at V-neck: on RS, k2tog, k1; on WS p1, p2tog.

To maintain the color pattern, you may need to work the Dec row in the final 3 sts on a knit row or the first 3 sts on a purl row.

Work 1 row even.

Repeat Dec row [every 2 rows, then every 4 rows] 8 times, then every 2 rows once—23 sts.

Work even until armhole is same length and row as Back.

Shape left shoulder

Bind off 4 sts at armhole edge 4 times.

Bind off remaining 7 sts.

Shape right V-neck

Return to 41 sts, RS facing.

Work 2 rows even.

Continue armhole shaping at same time as V-neck shaping.

Dec row Decrease in 3 sts at V-neck: on RS, k1, SSK; on WS, SSP, p1.

Repeat Dec row [every 2 rows, then every 4 rows] 8 times, then every 2 rows once—23 sts.

Shape right shoulder

Work as left shoulder.

SLEEVES

To make color pattern match at armhole, count down from armhole bind-off to determine where sleeves should begin in the color pattern (see page 72).

With any color, cast on 44 (44, 50, 50, 56) or 40 (40, 44, 44, 52) sts.

Work next 4 rows of color pattern.

Inc row Work 1, work lifted inc in next st (inc 1), work to last 2 sts, inc 1, work 1.

To maintain the color pattern, you might need to work the Inc row on the purl side (see lifted inc in purl, page 115).

Repeat Inc row every 8 (6, 6, 4, 4) rows 13 (16, 16, 20, 21) or 13 (16, 18, 22, 22) times more—72 (78, 84, 92, 100) or 68 (74, 82, 90, 98) sts.

Work even until Sleeve measures 16½", end with a WS row. SHORTEN OR LENGTHEN HERE

Shape cap

Bind off 3 (4, 6, 8, 10) sts at beginning of next 2 rows.

Dec row Work 1, SSK on RS (or p2tog on WS), work to last 3 sts, k2tog on RS (or SSP on WS), work 1.

Repeat Dec row every 2 rows 16 (18, 19, 21, 23) or 15 (17, 19, 21, 23) times more—32 or 30 sts.

Bind off 2 sts at beginning of next 2 rows, then bind off remaining sts.

FINISHING

Press or block pieces.

Sew shoulder seams.

Funnel neck only Sew funnel neck seams (if worked as 2 pieces).

Both versions Sew Sleeves into armholes.

Sew Sleeve and side seams.

V-neck edging With smaller needle and D, begin at right shoulder seam, pick up and knit as follows:

• 1 st for every bound-off st and 1 st for every 2-row step between bound-off sts at back neck curves;
• 1 st for every st on a holder;
• 4 sts for every 5 rows along V-neck diagonal.

Next rnd Bind off loosely.

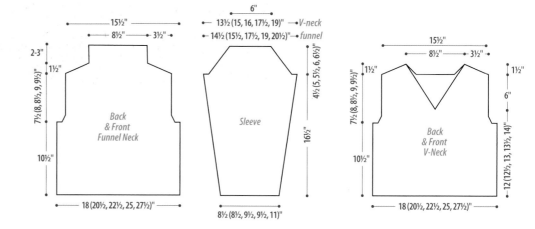

Page 52, M, Light weight: ELSEBETH LAVOLD
Cotton Patine 3 balls in 05 (A); 2 balls each in 12
(B), 02 (C), 03 (D), and 04 (E)
Right, M, Medium weight: JO SHARP
Classic DK Wool 3 balls in 327 (A); 2 balls each
in 344 (B), 346 (C), 901 (D), and 904 (E)

EXPERience
• *easy intermediate*
• *simple shaping*
• *mid-level finishing*

STANDARD FIT

S (M, L, 1X, 2X)

A 35½ (40, 44½, 49½, 54)"
B 20½ (21, 21½, 22, 22½)"
C 29 (29½, 30, 30½, 31)"

10cm/4"

24, 27
17, 18

• *over stockinette stitch*
• *using larger needles*

You'll need

1 2 3 **4** 5 6

• *Medium weight*

A • **490 (580, 680, 790, 1050) yds (sleeved)**

B • **290 (350, 410, 475, 540) yds (sleeved)**

A, B • **375 (450, 525, 610, 700) yds each (sleeved)**

C • **125 (150, 175, 200, 230) yds (sleeved)**

A, B • **135 (160, 190, 220, 250) yds each (sleeveless)**

C • **170 (200, 235, 270, 310) yds (sleeveless)**

I used

• *4.5mm/US7*

• *3.75mm/US5, 50cm/20"*

BROAD STRIPES

The striping of these garments evolved from looking through fashion magazines and then sketching and coloring. How could I use stripes to minimize width across the bust and add width at the shoulders? After this primary consideration, I wanted to play with stripes so that the knitting was still fun. How many colors and where to place them? I think the drawings and doodles actually took more time than the knitting!

Here's how the colors for the 2-color version were chosen:
• *main color, red (A);*
• *neutral color, oatmeal (B).*
If the main color is warm, pick a warm neutral; if the main color is cool, pick a cool neutral.

Here's how the colors for the 3-color version were chosen:
• *dark color (A)—in cotton, yellow-green; in mohair, very dark red-violet;*
• *light, neutral color (B)—in cotton, khaki; in mohair, off-white;*
• *bright color, close to the complementary of A (C)—in cotton, red; in mohair, orange.*

Notes
1 See *Skills-at-a-glance*, page 228, for SSK, slip stitch, k2tog, and lifted inc. **2** Work St st (knit on RS, purl on WS). **3** If you work as indicated, or only SHORTEN OR LENGTHEN where indicated, your stripes will match at the armhole. **4** The 3-color funnel is knit to 18 sts; the 2-color is knit to 17 sts. When 2 sets of numbers are given, the red are for funnel neck, the green are for V-neck. **5** See schematic page 54 with following changes: Front/Back to armhole is 11½", V-neck width is 8½", and sleeve width at underarm is 13½ (15, 17, 18½, 20)".

M, 18-st gauge:
ROWAN Kid Classic 3 balls each in 832 (A) and 828 (B); 1 ball in 827 (C)

BACK

With A, cast on 77 (87, 95, 107, 117) or 82 (92, 102, 114, 124) sts.
LENGTHEN HERE by adding A rows before working
color pattern.

The cotton version has 6 rows A added; the mohair version has 4.

Work color pattern as follows (each number equals the number of rows in that particular color):
[4A, 8B] 3 times—36 rows.
Carry color not in use up the side (page 70).
32A for versions with sleeves, 32C for version without sleeves.
Piece measures 11½".
SHORTEN HERE by subtracting A or C rows.

Shape armhole
Continue in color established for 6, (8, 10, 12, 14) more rows,
AT SAME TIME shape armhole as follows.
Bind off 3 (4, 6, 8, 10) sts at beginning of next 2 rows.
Sleeveless version only After armhole bind-off, sl 1 p-wise at beginning of every row until shoulder shaping.

This will make that edge tighter. Also, cut colors rather than carrying up armhole edge.

All versions: *Dec row* (RS) K1, SSK, work to last 3 sts, k2tog, k1.
Repeat Dec row every RS row 1 (5, 7, 11, 14) or 2 (6, 9, 13, 16) times more—67 or 70 sts.
AT SAME TIME, after broad stripe of A or C, work 18B, 18A, then B to end.
Work even until armhole measures 7½ (8, 8½, 9, 9½)", end with a WS row.

Shape shoulders
Funnel neck only Bind off 3 sts at beginning of next 10 rows—40 sts.

If you think you need a larger head opening, bind off fewer sts in the final shoulder bind off's.

With C, continue over remaining sts for 2–3".
Bind off very loosely.
V-neck only Bind off 3 sts at beginning of next 4 rows.
Right shoulder Bind off 3 sts at beginning of next RS row, work to 8 sts on right needle.
Turn, put center 33 sts on hold.
*Bind off 1 st at neck edge twice,
AT SAME TIME bind off 3 sts at armhole edge twice.
Left shoulder Return to 11 sts, RS facing.
Work 1 RS row.
Bind off 3 sts at armhole.
Work as right shoulder from* to end.

FRONT

Funnel neck only Work as Back to end.
V-neck only Work as Back until armhole measures 1½ (2, 2½, 3, 3½)", end with a WS row.
Shape left V-neck

Continue armhole Dec row and color pattern through neck shaping: color pattern from armhole is 6 (8, 10, 12, 14) A rows, 18B, 18A, then B to end.

Work 33 sts, put center st on holder.
Turn, work 1 WS row.
Dec row (RS) Work to last 3 sts, k2tog, k1.
*Repeat neck dec every RS row 17 times more—15 sts.
Work even until armhole measures 7½ (8, 8½, 9, 9½)", end with a WS row.
Shape left shoulder
Bind off 3 sts at armhole edge 5 times.
Shape right V-neck/shoulder
Return to 33 sts, RS facing.
Work 1 RS and 1 WS row.
Dec row (RS) K1, SSK, work to end.
Work as Left V-neck from* to end, but reverse shoulder shaping (by binding off on WS rows).

SLEEVES

With A or C, cast on 36 (36, 40, 40, 46) or 38 (38, 42, 44, 48) sts.
Work 4 A or C rows even.
For color pattern, see AT SAME TIME instruction below.
Inc row K1, work lifted inc in next st (inc 1), work to last 2 sts, inc 1, k1.
Repeat Inc row every 8 (6, 6, 4, 4) rows 10 (13, 15, 18, 19) times more—58 (64, 72, 78, 86) or 60 (66, 74, 82, 88) sts.
AT SAME TIME, work color pattern as follows:
V-neck only After initial 4 A rows, work 6 (8, 10, 12, 14) more rows—10 (12, 14, 16, 18) A.
SHORTEN OR LENGTHEN by adding or subtracting A rows.
Work [12B, 12A] 3 times.
Work 12 (12, 12, 12, 10) B.
Work 6 (4, 2, 0, 0) A.
Funnel neck only After initial 4 C rows, work 30 (32, 34, 36, 38) more rows—34 (36, 38, 40, 42) C.
SHORTEN OR LENGTHEN by adding or subtracting C rows.
Work [12A, 12B] 3 times, end with 6A (4A, 2A, 0A, 10B).
All versions

Piece measures 16½".

Shape cap

Color pattern changes to following through sleeve cap.
Work 6A (8A, 10A, 12A, 2B + 12A), then 18B, then A to end.
AT SAME TIME shape cap as follows.
Bind off 3 (4, 6, 8, 10) sts at beginning of next 2 rows.
Dec row K1, SSK, work to last 3 sts, k2tog, k1.
Repeat Dec row every RS row 12 (14, 16, 17, 19) or 12 (14, 16, 18, 19) times more—26 or 28 sts.
Bind off 2 sts at beginning of next 2 rows, then bind off remaining sts.

FINISHING

Sew shoulder seams.
Funnel neck only Sew funnel neck seams.
For all versions Sew Sleeves into armholes.
Sew Sleeve and side seams.
V-neck edging With smaller circular needle and A, begin at right shoulder seam, pick up and knit as follows:
- 1 st for every bound-off st and 1 st for every 2-row step between bound-off sts at back neck shaping;
- 1 st for every st on a holder;
- 4 sts for every 5 rows along V-neck diagonal.
  —approximately 124 sts.

Knit 1 rnd.
Final rnd, make loops Bind off across back neck. Bind off to 6 sts below left shoulder seam, (1 st on right needle).
Turn, *knit into st on left needle but do not remove st from needle, put new st onto left needle, pass old st over new st, repeat from* once more (1 loop made), turn.
(Bind off 7 more sts and repeat loop) until 5 loops on left neck edge.
Bind off to center front, count bound-off sts between final loop and center, then bind off same number of sts up right neck edge.
(Bind off 7 more sts and make loop) until 5 loops on right neck edge.
Bind off remaining sts.

Chain

Use approximately 7 yds A, doubled.
Crochet chain 60" long (see page 76).
Lace chain loosely through loops.

M, 18-st gauge:
MISSION FALLS 1824 Cotton 3 balls in 104 (B);
2 balls each in 304 (A) and 202 (C)

M, 17-st gauge: ROWAN Summer Tweed 5 balls in 537 (A),
3 balls in 508 (B)

EXPERience
- *intermediate*
- *basic lace pattern*
- *some shaping*

STANDARD FIT

S (M, L, 1X, 2X)

A 35½ (40, 44½, 49½, 54)"

B 20½ (21, 21½, 22, 22½)"

C 29 (29½, 30, 30½, 31)"

10cm/4"

28, 24
17
- *over lace pattern*
- *after blocking*
- *light yarn will get denser row gauge*

You'll need

3 OR 4

- *Light or Medium weight*
- *800 (900, 1020, 1140, 1260) yds*
- *965 (1050, 1200, 1330, 1470) yds*
- *divided between 3 or 5 colors*
- *may require more of darkest color*

I used

- *4m /US6*
- *4.5mm/US9*

M, Light weight: EUROFLAX Barcelona 2 skeins each in 2494, 2854, and 2894

WOBBLY STRIPES

It seemed I should not leave the subject of stripes without exploring it in something other than our standby stitch patterns. So, here's a piece done in a basic lace pattern. And isn't it interesting what happened to the stripes!

Choose 3 or 5 colors as follows:
- *mix of gray, taupe, and beige;*
- *shades from red to blue-violet.*

Notes
1 See *Skills-at-a-glance*, page 228, for yo, SSK, k2tog, and lifted inc. **2** See schematic, page 54 with following changes: sleeve width at cuff is 8½ (8½, 11, 11, 11)" and sleeve width at underarm is 14 (15, 16½, 18, 20)".

BACK/FRONT (MAKE 2)
With darkest color, cast on 77 (87, 97, 107, 117) sts. Work 16-row repeat of Lace A, begin with Row 1.
See reading charts (page 156), and managing stripes (page 70).
Change color every 8 rows to progressively lighter colors, then begin sequence again with darkest. Work until piece measures approximately 10½", end with Row 1 or 9.
SHORTEN OR LENGTHEN HERE
Note where armhole bind-off occurs in color sequence.
Shape armhole
Bind off 2 (4, 6, 8, 10) sts at beginning of next 2 rows. Work 1 WS row even.
Dec row (RS) K1, SSK, work to last 3 sts, k2tog, k1. Repeat Dec row every RS row 2 (5, 8, 11, 14) times more—67 sts.
In Rows 1–8 of the Lace charts, the lace unit is yo, k2tog; in Rows 9–16, the lace unit is SSK, yo. If the shaping involves a lace unit, do not work yo or lace decrease; just work the shaping decrease and knit the other stitch.
S, L, 2X only After 67 sts, work Lace B to shoulder.
M, 1X only Continue with Lace A to shoulder.

M, Medium weight: MOUNTAIN COLORS Mountain Goat 1 skein each in Deep Blue, Deep Purple, Mountain Twilight, Wild Raspberry, and Crazy Woman

Work even until armholes measure 7½ (8, 8½, 9, 9½)", end with a WS row.

Shape shoulders

Bind off 3 sts at beginning of next 10 rows—37 sts.

Neck

Work in pattern for 2–3".

S, L, 2X only Work Lace A.

M, 1X only Work Lace B.

Bind off all sts very loosely.

SLEEVES

See matching stripes, set-in sleeve (page 72), and schematic (page 54) to determine where to begin color pattern. Begin with Row 1 or 9 of Lace A.

Cast on 37 (37, 47, 47, 47) sts.

Work 4 rows in Lace A.

Inc row (RS) K1, work lifted inc in next st (inc 1), work to last 2 sts, inc 1, k1.

See note for lace units and dec's; treat inc's similarly.

Repeat Inc row every 8 (6, 6, 4, 4) rows 10 (12, 11, 14, 18) times more—59 (63, 71, 77, 85) sts.

Work to 16½", or desired length, end with Row 1 or 9 (as Front/Back).

Shape cap

Bind off 2 (4, 6, 8, 10) sts at beginning of next 2 rows.

Work 1 WS row even.

Dec row (RS) K1, SSK, work to last 3 sts, k2tog, k1.

Repeat Dec row every RS row 14 (14, 16, 17, 19) times more—25 sts.

Bind off 2 sts at beginning of next 2 rows, then bind off remaining 21 sts.

FINISHING

Press or block pieces.

Sew shoulder seams.

Sew funnel neck seams.

Sew Sleeves into armholes.

Sew Sleeve and side seams.

☐ *K on RS, p on WS*
◦ *Yo*
⟋ *K2tog*
⟍ *SSK*

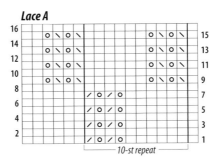

Lace A

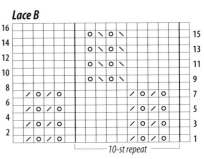

Lace B

EXPErience
- *easy intermediate*
- *simple shaping*
- *simple color changes*
- *simple finishing*

LOOSE FIT

Child's *6–8 (10–12)*

Man's *S (M, L, 1X, 2X)*

A *30½ (34, 40, 44, 48, 52, 56)"*

B *19 (22, 27, 28, 29, 30, 31)"*

C *22½ (26, 32, 33, 34, 35, 36)"*

10cm/4"

20

15

- *over stockinette stitch*
- *using larger needles*

You'll need

1 2 3 4 **5** 6

- *Bulky weight*

C1 • *360 (480, 600, 700, 800, 890, 990) yds*

C2 • *180 (240, 380, 420, 460, 520, 590) yds*

I used

- *6mm/US10*
- *4.5mm/US9*

50cm/20" long

Boy's 6–8: SCHEEPJESWOL Rigodon 4 balls in 515 (C1), 2 balls in 560 (C2)

GRADUATED STRIPES

This chapter really needed something for the guys—in colors, yarn and style that are all very easy and relaxed. There's no mystery to the color choices: just choose 2 that the guy in your life likes. For the man's, I chose colors to go with jeans; for the child's, I chose colors boys usually like.

Colors shown here are close to analogous (see page 10): yellow-green + blue and yellow-green + orange.

Notes
1 See *Skills-at-a-glance*, page 228, for lifted inc, and k2tog. *2* If only 2 numbers are given, the first is for Child's sizes, the second is for Man's.

BACK
With C1 and smaller needles, cast on 53 (59, 69, 77, 83, 89, 97) sts.

Work k1, p1 rib Begin and end RS rows with k1 and WS rows with p1. Work until rib measures 2 (3)", end with a RS row.

Next row (WS) Purl across, increasing evenly to 59 (65, 77, 85, 93, 99, 107) sts.

Change to larger needles and work St st to 32 (44, 44, 50, 56, 60, 64) rows C1.

SHORTEN OR LENGTHEN HERE

Work color pattern as follows.

When appropriate, carry all colors up the sides (page 70). Work on a circular needle so you can slip your work to the other end of the needle (see page 71).

**Work 1 row C2.

Work 7 (9) rows C1.

Work 2 (3) rows C2.

Work 6 (7) rows C1.

Work 4 rows C2.

Work 4 (6) rows C1.

Work 6 rows C2.

Man's L: SCHEEPJESWOL
Rigodon 9 balls in 515 (C1), 5 balls in 518 (C2)

Work 2 (4) rows C1.
Work 7 rows C2.**
Work 1 (3) rows C1.
Men's sizes only Work 9 rows C2.
Work 1 row C1.
All sizes Work remaining rows C2 until Back measures 18 (21, 26, 27, 28, 29, 30)", end with a WS row.
Shape right back neck Work 19 (22, 27, 31, 35, 38, 42) sts.
Put center 21 (23) sts on holder. Turn.
*Bind off 1 st at neck edge twice.
Work 2 RS rows even.
Bind off next RS row.
Shape left back neck Return to 19 (22, 27, 31, 35, 38, 42) sts, RS facing.
Work 2 rows.
Work as for right back neck from* to end, EXCEPT work WS rows even.

FRONT
Work as Back to 3" short of finished Back length, end with a WS row.
Shape left front neck
Work 24 (27, 32, 36, 40, 43, 47) sts.
Put center 11 (13) sts on holder. Turn.
*Bind off at neck edge 2 sts twice, 1 st 3 times.
Work even to same length as Back at shoulders, end with a WS row.
Bind off.
Shape right front neck
Return to 24 (27, 32, 36, 40, 43, 47) sts, RS facing.
Work 2 rows even.
Work as for left front neck from* to end.

SLEEVES
With C1 and smaller needles, cast on 25 (31, 35, 37, 37, 39, 39) sts.
Work k1, p1 rib Begin and end RS rows with k1 and WS rows with p1, until rib measures 2 (3)", end with a WS row.
Change to larger needles, and work St st to 4 rows.
Inc row (RS) K1, work lifted inc in next st (inc 1), work to last 2 sts, inc 1, k1.

Repeat Inc Row every 4 rows 14 (14, 17, 21, 24, 26, 29) times more—55 (61, 71, 81, 87, 93, 99) sts AT SAME TIME working color pattern as follows:
Work first 20 (32, 28, 28, 28, 28, 28) rows C1.
SHORTEN OR LENGTHEN HERE
Work color pattern as **to** for Back.
Work remaining rows C2 until Sleeve measures 15 (18, 22, 22, 22, 22, 22)", end with a WS row.
Bind off all sts.

FINISHING
Sew shoulder seams.
Neck edging
With C2 and smaller needle, begin at right shoulder seam, and pick up and knit as follows:
- 1 st for every bound-off st and 1 st for every 2-row step between bound-off sts at all neck shaping;
- 1 st for every st on a holder;
- 3 sts for every 4 rows along unshaped edges.
  —approximately 76 (80) sts.
This number must be divisible by 2. If needed, work p2tog at end of round.
Work 4 (6) rounds of k1, p1 rib.
Bind off.
Sew Sleeves into armholes.
Sew Sleeve and side seams.

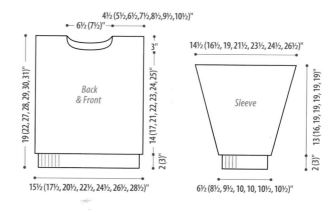

EXPERience
- *easy intermediate*
- *simple shaping*
- *mid-level finishing*

LOOSE FIT

S (M, L, 1X, 2X)

A *40 (44, 48, 52, 56)"*
B *20 (20½, 21, 21½, 22)"*
C *30 (30½, 31, 31½, 32)"*

10cm/4"

22, 26

14, 18

- over stockinette stitch
- using larger needles and main yarn

You'll need

2 + **3** OR **4**

- *Fine + Light weight*

OR

- *Medium weight*

OR

1 2 3 4 **5** 6

- *Bulky weight*

A • *1040 (1200, 1340, 1500, 1650) yds*

4 OR **5**

- *Medium or Bulky weight*

B, C • *140 (150, 165, 180, 195) yds each, for collar and cuffs*

B, C • *novelty yarns*

I used

- 4.5mm/US7 and 5.5mm/US9
- 3.75/US5 and 4.5mm/US7

- (optional) 5mm/H

- one–three 25mm/1" (optional)

- 76cm/30"
- 5.5mm/US9
- 4.5mm/US7

COLLAR-CLOSING CARDIGAN

With this garment, I wonder what's the most fun: picking the yarns, knitting it, or playing with the different ways to wear it. I hope you have the same 'This is *too* much fun!' experience.

To choose colors, find your main yarn first. Then find 2 other yarns—novelties with texture are preferred—with some of the main yarn's color(s). Try the wrapping-around-cardboard trick (on page 42) to check the combination.

Two gauges are offered. The red (Medium yarn) and the glitzy version (1 Fine + 1 Light yarn together) are worked at 18 sts. The softer yellow-green version (Bulky yarn) is worked at 14 sts.

The collars and cuffs are meant to be worn with the purl side showing. But if your main yarn is textured, and variegated, you will want the purl side as the right side of the main pieces also; the pattern changes slightly, and edgings are optional. For the lengthened version shown in color pages at the front of the book, add extra A yardage.

Stockinette stitch (St st)
RS rows Knit.
WS rows Purl.

Reverse Stockinette stitch (RSS)
RS rows Purl.
WS rows Knit.

Notes
1 See *Skills-at-a-glance*, page 228, for SSK, k2tog, and lifted inc. ***2*** When only 2 numbers appear, the first is for the 14-st gauge and the second is for the 18-st gauge.

BACK
For purl side facing, begin at Without edging.
With edging With smaller needles and A, cast-on 65 (70, 79, 84, 88) or 82 (90, 101, 108, 115) sts.

Begin with a knit row, work 4 rows St st.

Inc row (WS) Purl across, working lifted increase every 9 sts—
71 (77, 87, 93, 97) or 91 (99, 111, 119, 127) sts.

Without edging With smaller needles and A, cast on 71 (77, 87, 93, 97) or 91 (99, 111, 119, 127) sts.

Begin with a knit row, work 4 rows St st.

Both versions Change to larger needle, begin with a knit row, and work St st to 11", end with a purl row.

SHORTEN OR LENGTHEN HERE

Shape armhole

Bind off at beginning of next 2 rows 3 (3, 5, 7, 9) or 4 (5, 7, 9, 12) sts.

Dec row K1, SSK, work to last 3 sts, k2tog, k1.

Repeat Dec row every knit row 4 (7, 10, 11, 11) or 5 (8, 12, 14, 15) more times—55 or 71 sts,

*Work even until armhole measures 3 (3½, 4, 4½, 5)", end with a purl row.

Introduce collar yarns

If you prefer the purl side for the Body, you now need to 'switch sides' so the reverse side of the collar will show. If the next row would have been a knit, purl instead. Then work in St st as newly established.

Continue in St st as follows: work 1 row in first collar yarn (B), then 1 row in second collar yarn (C), then 1 row in A.

Continue for 5". Cut yarns, and put sts on holder.

LEFT FRONT

With edging Work as Back EXCEPT cast on 34 (36, 40, 42, 46) or 43 (46, 51, 55, 59) sts and increase to 37 (40, 44, 47, 51) or 47 (51, 56, 61, 65) sts.

Without edging Cast on 37 (40, 44, 47, 51) or 47 (51, 56, 61, 65) sts.

If the purl side is your right side, this will be your Right Front.

Both versions Change to larger needles and work St st to same length as Back to armhole, end with a purl row.

Shape armhole

Bind off at beginning of next row 3 (3, 5, 7, 9) or 4 (5, 7, 9, 12) sts.
Purl 1 row.

Dec row K1, SSK, knit to end.

Repeat Dec row every knit row 4 (7, 10, 11, 11) or 5 (8, 12, 14, 15) times more—29 or 38 sts,

Work as for Back from * to end.

RIGHT FRONT

Work as for Left Front but reverse shaping as follows:
Bind off for armhole on purl row, and work dec's on knit rows (knit to last 3 sts, k2tog, k1).

SLEEVES

Cuff

With smaller needles and A, cast-on 35 (35, 37, 37, 41) or 43 (43, 45, 45, 51) sts.

With edging Begin with a knit row, work 4 rows St st, then purl 1 row.

Without edging Knit 1 row, purl 1 row.

Both versions Change to larger needles.

Begin with a knit row, work St st, 1 row in each collar yarn then 1 row in A, to 6 rows.

Dec row K1, SSK, work to last 3 sts, k2tog, k1.

Repeat Dec row every 6 rows twice more—29 (29, 31, 31, 35) or 37 (37, 39, 39, 45) sts.

Work even to 6½".

Cut collar yarns.

Body

With A, continue in St st.

If you chose to work Front and Back with purl side showing, you now need to switch sides. If the next row would have been a knit, purl instead. Then work in St st as newly established.

Continue to 6 (4, 4, 4, 4) rows in A, end with a purl row.

Inc row K1, work lifted inc in next st (inc 1), knit to last 2 sts, inc 1, k1.

Repeat Inc row every 6 (5, 5, 4, 4) rows 11 (12, 14, 17, 18) or 14 (15, 19, 22, 23) times more—53 (55, 61, 67, 73) or 67 (69, 79, 85, 93) sts.

Work even until Sleeve measures 21" from beginning of cuff, end with a purl row.

SHORTEN OR LENGTHEN HERE

Shape cap

Bind off at beginning of next 2 rows—3 (3, 5, 7, 9) or 4 (5, 7, 9, 12) sts.

Dec row (RS) K1, SSK, knit to last 3 sts, k2tog, k1.

Repeat Dec row every RS row 12 (13, 14, 15, 16) or 15 (15, 18, 19, 20) times more—21 or 27 sts.

Bind off 2 sts beginning next 2 rows.

18-st gauge only Bind off 4 sts at beginning of next 2 rows.

All gauges Bind off remaining sts.

FINISHING

Mark center st of Sleeve cap. Work from both armholes towards this center st, sew Sleeve caps into armholes as follows:
  • sew 2 rows of Sleeve to 2 rows of Body,
  • sew 2 sts of Sleeve bind-off to 3 rows of body,
  • open sts of Front and Back will meet at center st of Sleeve cap.

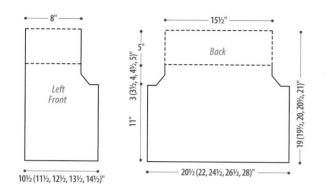

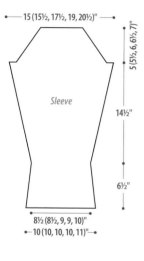

Left Front

8"

11"

10½ (11½, 12½, 13½, 14½)"

Back

15½"

5"

3 (3½, 4, 4½, 5)"

19 (19½, 20, 20½, 21)"

20½ (22, 24½, 26½, 28)"

Sleeve

15 (15½, 17½, 19, 20½)"

5 (5½, 6, 6½, 7)"

14½"

6½"

8½ (8½, 9, 9, 10)"

10 (10, 10, 11)"

If this did not work out quite right, rip back or add rows to Fronts and Back, but still end each piece with the same collar yarn.

Collar

Put 113 or 147 sts onto circular needle, placing markers as follows: at right shoulder, after next 27 or 35 back neck sts (before center st), and at left shoulder.

With RS facing and next yarn in sequence, work as follows:

Dec row Work to 3 sts before right-shoulder marker, SSK, k2, k2tog, work to 3 sts before center-Back marker, SSK, k1, knit center-Back st, k1, k2tog, work to 3 sts before left-shoulder marker, SSK, k2, k2tog, knit to end.

Working yarns in sequence, work 3 rows even.

Repeat these 4 rows 2 or 3 times more—95 or 123 sts.

Work even until collar measures 10", end with a purl row.

For body with purl side facing, go to Without edging.

With edging Change to smaller needles.

Dec row With main yarn, *k6, k2tog; repeat from* across row.

Work 3 rows RSS, then bind off all sts.

Sew edging down as invisibly as possible, because collar will be worn with both sides facing.

Without edging Change to smaller needles, and work St st in main yarn for 2 rows, then bind off all sts.

Both versions Sew side seams.

Sew Sleeve seams, taking only one-half stitch into seam allowance at cuff.

Front edgings (for fabrics with edgings)

Along Right Front edge, with RS facing, smaller needles, and main yarn, pick up and knit 3 sts for every 4 rows on main yarn then 5 sts for every 6 rows on collar yarns.

Work 4 rows RSS, then bind off all sts.

Work in same manner along Left Front edge.

Sew edgings down invisibly.

Front edgings (for fabrics without edgings)

If Front edge looks unfinished, with RS facing, use main yarn and crochet hook to single crochet (sc, see page 44) along edge of collar for both Right and Left Fronts. Add a second row of sc if desired.

Closures

Try garment on. See Wearing Suggestions.

If you need more than a shawl pin to hold collar in place, decide where you'd place 1–3 buttons, then make buttonloops as follows.

To close with 1, 2, or 3 buttons on Left Front, make button loops on Right Front as follows:

Button loops With RS facing, use main yarn and crochet hook. Leave 5" tail to back, draw yarn to front at edge of piece (1 loop on crochet hook). Chain (see page 76) 7 or 9 sts.
Cut yarn, and draw 5" tail through final chain.
Secure button loop(s) to edge of Right Front with tails.
Sew buttons to Left Front with desired overlap and to match placement of button loops.

Wrong-side button If you only used 1 button, or if your fabric is soft and you want to secure the left collar, add a wrong-side button as follows.
Make spot on RS of Left Front, about 1" from edge and in first row of collar yarns. Sew smaller button to this spot.
With desired overlap, find matching spot on WS of Right Front.
Force button through this spot on Right Front.
Reinforce this 'forced' buttonhole by stitching around it with main yarn.

Back tie If garment still does not feel secure, or you wish to wear with collar fully open, add a back tie as follows:
With main yarn doubled, crochet a chain 11" long (stretched).
Sew each end to inside Back armholes, 1" above introduction of collar yarns.

Wearing suggestions Try the portrait collar.
Try gathering the fabric at the neck and securing with a shawl pin.
Try folding the left collar edge under the right collar and letting the right collar drape over the shoulder.

Page 65, M: TAHKI Donegal Tweed 6 skeins in 840 (A); INTERLACEMENTS 1 skein each Periwinkle Petite in 216 (B) and Big Loop in 207 (C)
Above, M: 7 balls each LONDON YARNS Sinflex in 119 (A) and ROSINA Australian Merino Lame in 62 (A); 2 balls ROSINA Ker in 805 (B), 3 balls DALEGARN Ara in 21900 (C)
Below, S: PRISM Blossom three 8-oz skeins in Sagebrush (A); three 1-oz skeins each Bubbles in Nevada (B) and Lunette in Tumbleweed (C)

Managing Stripes

Stripes can be simple (2 rows in each of 2 colors) or complex (many colors, different numbers of rows in each). But, as mentioned in the introduction, stripes can pose issues. Here's how to deal with most of the issues expressed there. (Instructions for weaving in tails begin on page 73.)

CARRYING YARN UP THE SIDE

In a striped garment, we often don't need to cut the yarn every time we change color. But how far can we drag it up the side? And how do we not distort the fabric?

You'll have to make your own decision about how far you are comfortable dragging yarn to its next stripe. I will drag as much as 2", and here are two techniques to keep from distorting the sides of the garment.

For drags of 1" or less, you may do nothing. But you should stop after working 1–2 stitches of the new color to check for distortion. Or you may work as follows.

1 Lift the color you need to use over the color you have just used, ...

2 ...then bring the color you need to use from underneath and into working.

For drags of more than an inch, it can help to occasionally catch the not-in-use yarn by the yarn you are knitting with.

1 At the beginning of a row, pick up the color you need to use later (the blue), take it over the color you will use next (the white), then proceed to work that next color.

If you've knit something in stripes and are not happy with the result, you might be able to overdye it. See Oops!, page 224, and check out the other rescue possibilities for common mistakes.

If you drag a yarn farther than you think you should, and have loops of yarn at the edge of your piece that you are afraid will catch on stuff, you can secure them in the seam.

Even though I don't mind weaving in tails, I drag colors up the side whenever possible. But I never drag color up the side if that edge is not going to be finished. In other words, I don't drag color for a striped scarf, and I did not drag color along the armhole of the Broad Stripes sleeveless (page 56).

This same principle of dragging applies to shoulder bind-off's. If reasonable, drag the color from the armhole edge to the next bind-off, being careful not to pull too tightly. Long strands of color can be secured in the shoulder seams.

EVEN OR ODD ROWS OF COLOR

Even rows of a color are fairly straightforward. If a color is used over an even number of rows, when you are done with it the alternate color will be at that edge ready to knit the next row as usual.

Odd rows of a color have added complexity. If a color is used over an odd number of rows, when you are done with it an alternate color may be at the other end of the knitting. In this situation, work on a circular needle. This allows you to slide the work to the other end of the needle, where the yarn is waiting. But this does mean that if the fabric is stockinette stitch, you could have 2 knit rows (2 RS rows) or 2 purl rows (2 WS rows) in sequence.

Working 2 RS or 2 WS rows in sequence is not a difficult concept through straight pieces. But once shaping is introduced, you might find yourself needing to work an armhole decrease (usually worked as an SSK or k2tog on alternate RS rows) on a wrong-side row (as an SSP or p2tog). (The patterns of this chapter have detailed instructions for this possibility.)

This management of color over odd numbers of rows becomes near-impossible across shoulder bind-offs, so here's when you cut your yarns and only work 1 RS row followed by 1 WS row, etc.

STRIPES THROUGH INC'S AND DEC'S

Whether stripes are simple or complex, there will be times in the pattern when you are asked to do 2 things at once: manage the colors *plus* work increases or decreases. For some patterns (regular stripes of 2 or 4 rows), this won't be a challenge. But once the stripes become irregular or are worked over odd numbers of rows, the challenge increases.

You'll want to find a way to keep track of your work. Here's a simple one.
- Write out your color sequence.
- Note which rows involve inc's or dec's.
- Cross rows off as you work them.

It may seem unnecessary work to keep track of inc's and dec's through stripes, but imagine the following scenario. You put your knitting down, return to it later, and wonder 'What color's next? And do I decrease on this row or not?" If you have to puzzle this out every time, this knitting might become one of those UFO's (unfinished objects) knitters feel guilty over. It's my intention to help you minimize these!

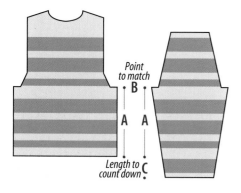

Point
to match
• B •

A A

Length to
count down • C •

Matching stripes

Sometimes we want stripes to match on a sweater; if they don't, we think the work looks unprofessional. Where do we want them to match, and how do we make it happen?

IN A SET-IN SLEEVE OR RAGLAN GARMENT

In a set-in sleeve garment, we might choose to have the stripes match across the chest. Since the sleeves are usually longer than the body (A on drawing), this means that we cannot assume that we can just begin the sleeves at the same point in the stripe pattern as the body. What we do know is that we want to arrive at the same point in the stripe pattern for the armhole bind-offs in both pieces (B on drawing). So, now we can figure out where to start the stripe pattern for the sleeve (C on drawing).

- Determine how much longer the sleeve needs to be than the body. (If the body is 11" to the armhole, and the sleeve is 16", the difference is 5".)
- Translate this number of inches into rows. (If your gauge is 6 rows to the inch, 5" × 6 rows = 30 rows.)
- Find the point in the stripe pattern at which the body began. (Let's assume the body began on row 1.)
- Count backwards in the stripe pattern to the number of rows calculated above. (In a 12-row repeat, 30 rows = 12 + 12 + 6. If 6 rows still need to be done in a 12-row repeat, you need to start your sleeve on row 7 of the pattern.)

IN A DROP-SHOULDER GARMENT

The stripes don't match up in a drop shoulder garment the same way they do in a set-in sleeve. And it's pretty difficult to know exactly where a stripe in the sleeve will fall relative to a stripe in the body, because we don't always know where the seam will fall on the arm. So I think you can pretty much do whatever you want and not worry about trying to match anything.

Weaving in tails

You can 'knit tails in'—knit 5 or more stitches with both the old and the new tails. While this works well at the join of 2 balls of the same-color yarn, it's not the best method when the tails are different colors. Here we need to do something different.

One method is to 'weave' in a tail, as you knit. It's an important skill—weaving in the tails as you go, rather than sewing them in later—so over the next 2 pages, I offer 3 methods of doing this. (While they are all worked slightly differently, the result is the same.) Choosing one and mastering it will make your multi-colored knitting ever so much more enjoyable. But before looking at specific methods, some general concepts should be addressed.

When changing colors in knitting, 2 'tail' situations present: the first is the beginning tail of that color, which you will weave over a subsequent row in that color; the second is the final tail of that color, which you will weave over the first row of the next color. I know this latter suggests that the first color will peek through the second, but it won't.

Sometimes this weaving-in-of-tails is the best possible method to use even when the tails are the same color. It depends upon the yarn and the stitch pattern. What's important is to have more than one method at your disposal and to choose the best for the situation.

The green tail was just woven over the first row of white (and needs to be trimmed). See lower in the swatch where a green tail was woven and where a white tail was woven.

On the right side, none of these woven tails are visible.

So, here's how I find this works best:
• never weave the tail of a color over the first row in which it is introduced;
• over row 1 of the new color, weave the final tail of the color you just finished working with;
• over row 3 of the new color, weave its beginning tail;
• over row 1 of the next color, weave the final tail of the color you just finished working with.
And so on....

WORKING YARN IN RIGHT HAND, TAIL IN LEFT / KNIT SIDE

For this method of weaving, I think it helps to realize that you never wrap the tail around the right needle. Rather, you could visualize it as follows: first, you knit under the tail, so you have to lift it; next, you knit over the tail, so you have to let it fall.

This method of weaving is shown over knit rows. It is possible to do it over purl rows also. Just do everything as written here, but insert the needle as if to purl and wrap the yarn as if to purl.

1 Holding the working yarn in the right, knit the first stitch as usual.

2 Insert right needle into next stitch as usual.

3 With left hand, lift tail of old color over right needle so it sits parallel to left needle.

WORKING YARN IN LEFT HAND, TAIL IN RIGHT / KNIT SIDE

While this method of weaving feels very different from the other two, it gives the same result.

The little jingle that goes with this method is 'wrap, wrap, un-wrap.'

This method does not work on the purl side.

1 Holding the working yarn in the left hand, knit the first stitch as usual.

2 Insert right needle into next stitch as usual.

3 Wrap the tail around the right needle (as if you were knitting with yarn in the right hand).

4 Wrap the yarn around the right needle (as if you were knitting with the yarn in the left hand).

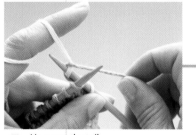

5 Un-wrap the tail.

6 Pull the yarn through to make the stitch as usual.

7 Knit next stitch on left needle as usual, without engaging the tail. Repeat Steps 2–7 until you have woven over 8–10 sts.
If tail is visible to front of work, pull slightly to tighten.
Never trim tail to less than ½".

4 Knit next stitch on left needle as usual, without engaging the tail.

5 Let tail fall, and knit subsequent stitch on left needle as usual.

Repeat Steps 2–5 until you have woven over 8–10 stitches.
If tail is visible to front of work, pull slightly to tighten.
Never trim tail to less than ½".

WORKING YARN AND TAIL BOTH IN LEFT HAND / KNIT SIDE

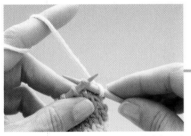

1 Holding the working yarn in the left hand, knit the first stitch as usual.

2 Insert right needle into next stitch as usual.

3 Pick up tail with thumb and third finger of left hand, and lift tail over right needle so it sits parallel to left needle.

4 Knit next stitch on left needle as usual.

5 Hold tail down with left middle finger, then knit next stitch as usual, without engaging tail.
Repeat Steps 2–5 until you have woven 8–10 sts.
If tail is visible to front of work, pull slightly to tighten.
Never trim tail to less than ½".

For this method of weaving, I think it helps to remember that you do not wrap the tail around the right needle. Rather, you could visualize it as follows: first, you knit under the tail, so you have to lift it; next, you knit over the tail, so you have to let it fall.

This method of weaving is shown over knit rows. It is possible to do it over purl rows also. Just do everything as written here, but insert the needle as if to purl, and wrap the yarn as if to purl.

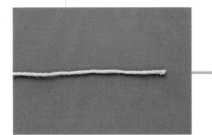

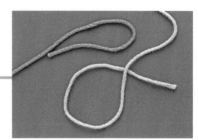

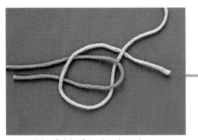

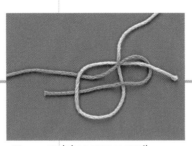

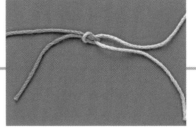

Weaver's knot

Here's a tiny tight knot that you can knit right over. Sometimes, when all other methods of joining one ball of yarn to another are more visible, this can be the right choice.

Sometimes, when knitting motifs of pre-measured lengths of yarn, we find ourselves 4–6" short of yarn. I would almost always choose to knot rather than weave in yet 2 more tails over a short stretch of knitting.

To make this easier to see, I show one tail in green and one in white. In your work, both tails would be the same color.

I also find this easiest to demonstrate with the tails lying flat on a table. Once you master the knot, you won't find it difficult to do in your hands.

1 Lay 1 tail pointing east.

2 Take yarn south, then north, over tail. (A circle is formed.)

3 Take 2nd tail and fold.

4 Take fold of 2nd tail under west side of circle… over east side of circle,

5 …and then over east tail.

6 Bring matching tails and yarns together, …

7 …and pull against each other to tighten. Do not cut tails shorter than ½".

Crocheted chain

I suggest a crocheted chain to hold the back of the Collar-closing cardigans together and to make button loops for these garments. I am sure you can find other uses for it. Toggles for buttons? Embellishments?

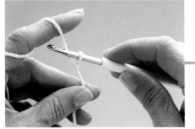

1 Make a slip knot and put it onto a crochet hook. Hold yarn and tail in left hand.
2 Take crochet hook to left of yarn,…

3 …then behind yarn,…

4 …then draw yarn through loop on hook.

Repeat Steps 2–4 to desired length. Cut yarn and bring through loop on hook to finish.

LEARNING, REMEMBERING, RE-LEARNING

I was the study skills advisor at a Canadian university, teaching—among other things—learning and remembering. As I prepared for this position, I was surprised by what I did not know about a subject so central to our lives. How do we learn? How do we remember what we learn? And how do we un-learn stuff that no longer serves us?

First, we take in new information. But this isn't learning; all we do is hold it in short-term memory. We don't actually learn until the material is transferred to long-term memory.

When does this transfer occur? It happens when we stop taking in new information. As long as we are taking in new stuff, nothing much more than temporary storage occurs. And, unfortunately, our temporary storage facility—short-term memory—is limited. It's entirely possible to work too hard, to over-fill it—kinda like pouring water into a jar that is already over-flowing. Short-term memory is filled in 50 minutes, and after that, we need to take a 10-minute break. What to do during the break, while material is being transferred to long-term memory? Nothing much: look out the window, eat ice cream, go for a walk, listen to music, knit!

While we're taking a break, the new piece of information is transferred to long-term memory, in a manner best understood with the analogy of the brain as a bowl of jelly (feels like it some days, doesn't it!). A new piece of information is like a trickle of hot water through this bowl of jelly. But, like jelly, the track would soon close over unless we were to trickle more hot water, at regular intervals, until we had engraved a permanent track. To remember this new piece of information, we must retrieve it regularly—sending trickles of hot water down the track within 24 hours, then again in a week, in a month, and finally in 6 months. Now it's ours!

But, learning a new knitting skill isn't mastered by just thinking about it, is it? No, memory isn't only in the brain. It is it a fluid thing, coursing through the entire body. That's why we hear of muscle memory (as we learn a new knitting skill) or cellular memory (of traumatic experiences held in the body).

Much of our lives is spent trying to remember stuff. Usually it's good stuff that we want to remember—the periodic table, a language, how to knit, how to play a Chopin Nocturne. But the other side to this coin is how hard it is to reject stuff—things taught or experienced for which we might have deeply-grooved neural pathways or for which we have etched-by-adrenalin cellular memory.

One of my favorite quotes is "The hardest practices to break are the ones we take for granted." It is difficult to challenge assumptions with which we have lived our lives, deeply-engraved truths we hold sacred, ways of living upon which we are convinced our survival depends.

How do we take no practices for granted? As knitters, it might mean taking the risk of knitting a garment in the color other than the one in which it is shown. As citizens, it might mean challenging how things are normally done. As victims of unhappy early experience, it explains why therapy is so difficult—addressing and releasing the permanent messages etched into our cells, then doing the work of forging new neural pathways.

Given how essential memory is to our lives, isn't it amazing how little we know about it and how rarely we challenge it as a determinant of behavior?

STRIPES THAT AREN'T

The last chapter was dedicated to stripes. And as complex as they became in terms of choosing colors, matching colors, color repeats, carrying the yarn up the side, how to minimize the 'wide' factor, they were pretty simple to knit: 1 or more rows A, 1 or more rows B, etc.

This chapter explores the knitting of stripes that don't *look* like stripes. In other words, these stitch patterns really are just stripes (some rows A followed by some rows B, usually no more than 2 colors). But they involve a simple manipulation of a stitch (by slipping or dipping, by increasing or decreasing) to produce a fabric that may look quite complex, quite intricate, and anything but what it is—pretty much just simple stripes.

In their simplest incarnation, these fabrics not only don't look like stripes but don't have any of the complex issues of stripes (as outlined in the first paragraph). They just do their thing while you do yours, all the while looking like a knitting genius!

These truly are the kind of big-bang-for-your-buck stitch patterns that I constantly return to and always fall back upon when I want to re-establish my love for knitting at its simplest, most rhythmic, most effective. With these stitch patterns, I know I can combine colors or textures to produce integrated, interesting fabrics that I am sure to love. Hope you love 'em too!

Chapter Three

The Patterns

Additional Skills

EXPerience
- *easy*
- *garter stitch*
- *simple finishing*

Scarf 6×92"
Afghan 48" square

10cm/4"

16

16

- *approximate gauge*
- *over garter stitches and ridges (knit every row)*
- *before fulling*

You'll need

1 2 3 **4** 5 6

- **Medium weight**
- **For scarf**
- **D1, D2 • 95 yds each**
- **L1, L2 • 95 yds each**
- **A • 40 yds**
- **For afghan**
- **D1–6, L1–6, A, E • 220 yds each**

I used

- **5mm/US8**

- **5mm/US8**
- **two, 72cm/29"**

CYNTHIA'S SCARF/AFGHAN

This piece is based on the log cabin quilt pattern, introduced to me by my mother-in-law and so named for her. It's also an example of 'modular' knitting: we knit a form (a module), repeat it, then attach a number of modules to form a scarf, an afghan, the body of a sweater.

It won't take much study of modules before you understand how one (the square offered here) could be adapted and inserted into another modular pattern (say Nod-to-Mod, the next pattern in this book). And it won't take much experience of these before you're quite addicted!

Here's how the variegated colors were chosen for the scarf.
- *Pick something strong (traditionally red, but I liked chartreuse) for the center (A).*
- *Pick 2 dark colors (D1 and D2). I used brown & dark green.*
- *Pick 2 light colors (L1 and L2). I used pale gray and pale green.*

Here's how the colors were chosen for the afghan.
- *Pick something warm (traditionally red or orange, symbolizing the hearth) for the center (A).*
- *Pick up to 6 dark colors (D1–6). I used brown, dark green, another dark green, olive green, bright green, and dark rust.*
- *Pick up to 6 light colors (L1–6). I used off-white, turquoise, light green, flesh, pale yellow, lilac.*
- *Pick one more dark color, which could be one already used, for the edging (E). I used eggplant.*

I fulled the afghan, which made it 9" smaller in both directions.

Notes
1 See *Skills-at-a-glance*, page 228, for e-wrap cast-on, 3-needle bind-off, and fulling. **2** Put stitches on hold (hold sts) by binding off with waste yarn (see page 115) or putting stitches onto thread or holder. **3** When 2 sets of instructions are given, the first is for the scarf, the second for the afghan.

Afghan: PATONS Classic Wool 1 ball each 238 (A), 227 (D1), 220 (D2), 221 (D3), 205 (D4), 240 (D5), 206 (D6), 202 (L1), 236 (L2), 222 (L3), 232 (L4), 203 (L5), 237 (L6), 231 (E)

LOG CABIN SQUARE

1 With A, e-wrap cast on 8 sts. Knit 16 rows.

I recommend the e-wrap cast-on, because it is easy to pick up and knit from.

Cut yarn at end of each color section.

Work final tail of previous color over first row of new color. Work initial tail of new color over third row of new color (page 73).

2 With L1, knit 8 rows. Hold sts.

For all turns, turn piece 90 degrees to right.

Work all pick up's as follows:

- slip left needle from left to right through garter ridges (or cast-on stitches, or stitches on hold) at edge of piece.
- the number means how many stitches are picked up; the letter is the color of the picked-up stitches (8A, 4L means pick up 8 sts from A edge and 4 sts from L edge).

3 Turn, pick up 8A, 4L. With L2, knit 8 rows. Hold sts.

Be sure to pick up the same part of every edge st along garter ridges.

4 Turn, pick up 8A, 4L. With D1, knit 8 rows. Hold sts.

5 Turn, pick up 4L, 8A, 4D. With D2, knit 8 rows. Hold sts.

6 Turn, pick up 4L, 8L, 4D. With L2, knit 8 rows. Bind off (hold sts).

7 Turn, pick up 4D, 12L, 4L. With L1, knit 8 rows.

Hold sts (for scarf leave a long tail).

8 Turn, pick up 4D, 12D, 4L. With D2, knit 8 rows. Bind off (hold sts).

9 Turn, pick up 4L, 16D, 4D. With D1, knit 8 rows. Hold sts (for scarf leave a long tail).

Afghan only

10 Turn, pick up 4L, 16L, 4D. With L5, knit 8 rows. Hold sts.

11 Turn, pick up 4D, 20L, 4L. With L6, knit 8 rows. Hold sts.

12 Turn, pick up 4D, 20D, and 4L. With D5, knit 8 rows. Hold sts.

Turn, pick up 4L, 24D, and 4D. With D6, knit 8 rows. Hold sts.

13 **Scarf only** Make 6 squares as written.

Make 5 more squares, but reverse L1 and L2 and D1 and D2.

Afghan only Make 36 squares.

Choose lights and darks randomly, but do not place a color adjacent to itself.

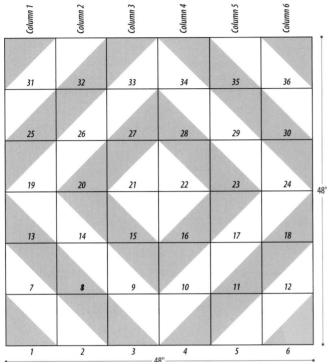

Scarf: 1 ball each JO SHARP Rare
Comfort 613 (A), 611 (L1), 612 (D1),
615 (L2), 616 (D2)

Scarf Squares

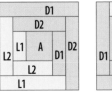

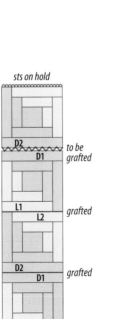

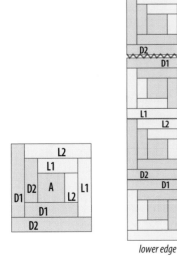

FINISHING / SCARF
Assembly
- alternate squares as shown in diagram, joining light edges to light (or dark to dark);
- graft squares together.

While these squares were knit in garter stitch, I did not set them up for grafting in garter; graft in stockinette stitch.

Block.

FINISHING / AFGHAN

Use diagram for placement of light versus dark.

Pick squares to be 1 and 7. Orient them according to diagram.

With left needle and working from left to right along square 1, pick up 4 sts along all row edges, and pick up all live sts—32 sts.

Use a second needle to pick up in same manner along edge of square 7.

With RS's together and working loosely, use an appropriately colored piece to join squares with 3-needle bind-off.

I used 3-needle bind-off for stability.

Now join square 7 to 13 in same manner.

Continue until first column is joined.

Work columns 2–6 in same manner.

Using circular needles, join columns together in same manner.

With tails, sew closed any holes.

Edging

Start at any corner with a circular needle. Pick up in same manner along one edge of the afghan—192 sts

With E, knit 6 rows, then bind off.

*Turn, and work in same manner along next edge, adding 3 sts for previous edging.

Knit 6 rows, then bind off.

Repeat from *.

(Optional) Full.

EXPERience

- *intermediate*
- *mid-level stitch pattern*
- *simple shaping*

LOOSE FIT

23-st gauge piece
S *(M, L, 1X, 2X)*
A *42 (45, 48, 52, 56)"*
B *20½ (21½, 22, 22½, 23)"*
C *29½ (30, 30½, 31, 31½)"*
14-st gauge piece
S–M *(L–1X, 2X+)*
A *48 (54, 60)"*
B *23"*
C *31"*

10cm/4"

23, 14
23, 14

- *over garter stitches and ridges*
- *after blocking*

You'll need

2 OR **5**

- *Fine weight*
D1 • *715 (785, 855, 950, 1045) yds*
D2 • *665 (730, 795, 880, 970) yds*
CC • *350 yds*
- *Bulky weight*
MC • *900 (1020, 1125) yds*
CC • *325 yds*
- *variegated yarns*

I used

- *3.5mm/US4*
- *5mm/US8*

- *3.5mm/US4*
- *5mm/US8*
50cm/20"

&

- *stitch markers*
- *waste yarn (similar weight) optional*

NOD-TO-MOD PULLOVER

It would be difficult to write a book on color without giving a 'nod to mod'—attention to modular knitting. It's a wonderful technique—knitting a module (a square, a triangle, a shell shape) that is repeated and (usually) attached to other modules as it is knit. The result is something that looks oh-so-complex but need not be. (Cynthia's scarf is made of very simple modules.)

Whether simple or complex, modular knitting is also what I call 'order-in-Chinese-for-dinner' knitting. *"I'll start dinner after I finish this square…or maybe after I start the next square." Repeat from * until it's take-out time again!

The mohair piece is knit to 14 sts; the colors are a shade of red-violet (MC)+a lighter tone of an analogous red-orange (CC). The finer piece is knit to 23 sts; the colors are 2 dark variegated greens (D1, D2)+a complementary variegated red (CC).

The sleeves for either may be knit in Zig Zag Lace or Garter stitch.

The first half of the square module is worked by shortening rows—leaving stitches behind and decreasing at center. The second half is worked by lengthening rows—bringing stitches back into working and increasing at center. The decreases and increases make the rows of knitting miter (turn a corner).

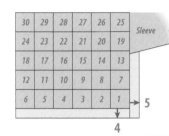

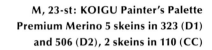

Short-row square

Weave all tails over next (long-enough) RS row (see page 73).

1 **Decrease miter**

Row 1, short row (RS) With MC (D1), k12 (20), place marker (pm), k11 (19), turn—1 st left behind (1B).

Row 2, short row K22 (38), turn—1B.

Note that the RS and WS short rows are a pair, each leaving the same number of stitches unworked at turning.

Row 3, *short row+decrease* Knit to 2 sts before marker, k2tog, SSK, k8 (16), turn—2B.

WS rows Knit 4 fewer sts than previous WS row, turn, leave 1 more behind each time.

RS rows Decrease as Row 3 at center, then k2 fewer than previous RS row and leave 1 more behind each time.

Fine gauge only Cut D1 at end of Row 8, introduce CC in Row 9.

Center

Bulky gauge only: *Row 11* End with k0, turn—6B.

Row 12 K2, turn—6B. Cut MC.

Row 13 With CC, k2, turn—6B.

Fine gauge only: *Row 20* End with k2, turn—10B.

Row 21 K2, turn—10B.

2 **Increase miter**

Work all slips as follows: with yarn in front, slip 1 purlwise.

Row 14 (22), add row (WS) K2, sl 1, turn.

Row 15 (23), add row+increase Knit to 1 st before marker, kf&b twice, k1 (bring 1 into working), turn.

WS rows K4 more than previous WS row and bring 1 more into working each time.

RS rows Increase at center as Row 15 (23), then k2 more than previous RS row and bring 1 more into working each time.

Fine gauge only Cut CC at end of Row 34, introduce D1 Row 35.

Row 23 (39) Increase at center, k9 (17), turn—1 st remains.

Row 24 (40) K22 (38), sl 1, turn—0 sts remain.

Cut CC (D2).

Piece measures 4 (3½)" square.

M, 23-st: KOIGU Painter's Palette Premium Merino 5 skeins in 323 (D1) and 506 (D2), 2 skeins in 110 (CC)

sts on hold

3 Sts for Square 2 / Square 1 / Cast-on Sts

2

1

↑ *Direction of knitting*
● *Increase*
● *Decrease*

Zig Zag Lace

16 | | | | | | | o | / | 15
14 | | | | | | | o | / | 13
12 | | | | | | o | / | | 11
10 | | | | | o | / | | | 9
8 | | | \ | o | | | | | 7
6 | | \ | o | | | | | | 5
4 | \ | o | | | | | | | 3
2 | \ | o | | | | | | | 1

9-st repeat

16-row repeat

☐ K on RS
▦ K on WS
o Yo
╱ K2tog
╲ SSK

Notes

1 See *Skills-at-a-glance*, page 228, for e-wrap cast on, SSK, k2tog, slip stitch, kf&b, yo, and grafting. *2* When only 2 numbers or colors appear, the first is for the bulky gauge and the second for the fine gauge. *3* Put sts on hold by binding off with waste yarn (see page 115) or putting sts onto thread or holder.

FRONT / BACK (MAKE 2)
Rectangle

All sizes begin with rectangles made as follows. Pieces are made wider (for larger sizes) after sleeves are attached.
With MC (D1), cast on *12 (20) sts, pm, repeat from* to 84 (140) sts.

I recommend the e-wrap cast-on, because it is easy to pick up and knit from.

Square 1
Work short-row square from first 24 (40) cast-on sts.
After Row 24 (40) Put first 12 (20) sts on hold, remove marker.

Squares 2–6
Row 1 K12 (20) sts from end of previous square, pm, then k11 (19) sts from cast-on.
After Row 24 (40) Put first 12 (20) sts on hold, remove marker, bind off final 12 (20) sts with CC (D2).

Square 7
Row 1 With MC (D1), cast on 12 (20) sts onto left needle. K12 (20) sts, pm, k11 (19) sts from top of square below (in this case, Square 1).
After Row 24 (40) Put first 12 (20) sts on hold, remove marker.

Squares 8–12, 14–18, 20–24
Work as Squares 2–6.

Squares 13, 19
Work as Square 7.
SHORTEN by 4 (3½)" by eliminating 19–24.
LENGTHEN by 4 (3½)" by repeating 19–24.
There will be an opportunity to lengthen by less than this at the end of these pieces: see Additional Lengthening.

Squares 25 (26–30)
Work as Square 7 (2–6) to end of Row 24 (40). Do not cut CC (D2); bind off first 12 (20) sts with CC (D2).

Additional lengthening
Fine gauge only Along bottom edge and with D1, pick up and knit 1 st for every cast-on st—120 sts. Knit to 0 (1, 1½, 2, 2½)", then bind off.
SHORTEN OR LENGTHEN HERE
I added nothing to the bulky garment, but it could be lengthened in the same manner, with MC.

LEFT SLEEVE
Body
With MC (D1) cast on 36 or 45 (45, 54, 54, 63) sts for fine gauge.
Fine gauge only Work 1 row D1, *2 rows D2, 2 rows D1, repeat from* for duration of Sleeve.
All gauges Work Zig Zag Lace or Garter stitch to 2".
Inc row K1, kf&b, work to last 2 sts, kf&b, k1.
Work 3 or 5 (5, 3, 3, 3) rows even.
Repeat Inc row every 4 or 6 (6, 4, 4, 4) rows 13 (16, 20) or 26 (30, 32, 36, 36) times more—64 (70, 78) or 99 (107, 120, 128, 137) sts.
Work even until Sleeve measures 18 or 18 (18½, 19, 19½, 20)".
SHORTEN OR LENGTHEN HERE
Saddle
At beginning of next 2 rows, bind off 21 (24, 28) or 32 (36, 42, 46, 51) sts—22 or 35 (35, 36, 36, 35) sts.
Work even until saddle measures 8½ (7)", end with a RS row. Through neck shaping, discontinue lace and work in garter.
Front neck shaping
Over next WS row, work 11 (17) sts.
Turn, and bind off 4 (6) sts at beginning of next RS row.
Work 1 WS row.
At beginning of following RS rows, bind off 2 sts once, 1 st twice, 3 sts once or 3 sts once, 2 sts once, 1 st 3 times, 3 sts once.
Back neck shaping
Return to remaining sts, WS facing.
Bind off 1 st at beginning of next 2 (3) WS rows, then work remaining sts even until back neck measures 3½", end with a WS row.
Put sts on holder.

RIGHT SLEEVE
Work as Left sleeve to front neck shaping, then reverse shaping.
Shape front neck by binding off on WS rows and back neck by binding off on RS rows.

FINISHING
Begin at upper corners of Back, match to corner of Sleeves (at bind off).
The seaming ratios offered work if your stitch and row gauges match mine.
Sew Sleeve saddles across upper Back as follows:
6 sts to 5 ridges or 7 sts to 8 ridges.
Add or subtract rows on back saddles so live sts meet at center Back. Graft live sts together.

Graft in St st and pull grafting thread tight to form seam with no seam allowance.

Sew Sleeve saddles down sides of Back as follows:

7 sts of garment edge to 6 sts of Sleeve bind-off or 1 st of garment edge to 1 st of Sleeve bind-off.

Begin at upper corners of Front, match to corner of Sleeves (at bind off). Seam pieces as above.

Saddles will end approximately 2" from center Front.

5 **Widening for larger sizes**

Along right side of Front below Sleeve and with MC (D1), pick up and knit 1 st for every remaining cast-on st.

Fine gauge, M (L, 1X, 2X) Knit to ¾ (1½, 2½, 3½)". Bind off.

Bulky gauge, L–1X (2X+) Knit to 1½ (3)". Bind off.

Do the same along left side of Front.

Do the same widening to both sides of the Back.

Sew Sleeve seams.

Sew side seams, leaving 3-4" open at lower edge if desired.

Neck edging

With MC or (D1 or D2) and circular needle, begin at center back neck, pick up and knit as follows:

- 2 sts for every 3 ridges across back;
- 5 (7) sts at back neck shaping;
- 1 st for every bound-off st at front neck shaping;
- 1 st for every bound-off st at open space of center front.

Purl 1 round.

Bind off.

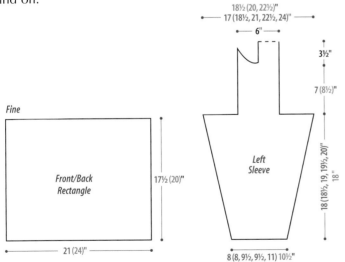

Fine

Front/Back Rectangle — 17½ (20)" — 21 (24)"

Left Sleeve — 18½ (20, 22½)" — 17 (18½, 21, 22½, 24)" — 6" — 3½" — 7 (8½)" — 18 (18½, 19, 19½, 20)" — 18" — 8 (8, 9½, 9½, 11) 10½"

S–M, 14-st: ARTFUL YARNS Portrait 6 balls in 101 (MC) and 2 balls in 114 (CC)

EXPErience

- *easy intermediate*
- *repetitive stitch pattern*
- *simple finishing*

Width 27"
Length 90"

10cm/4"

22 ▦
15

- *over Houndstooth*
- *after blocking*

You'll need

1 2 3 **4** 5 6

- *Medium weight*
  MC • 920 yds
  CC1–7 • 100 yds each color

I used

- *5mm/US8*

- *5mm/US8, 75cm/30"*

- *4.5mm/G*

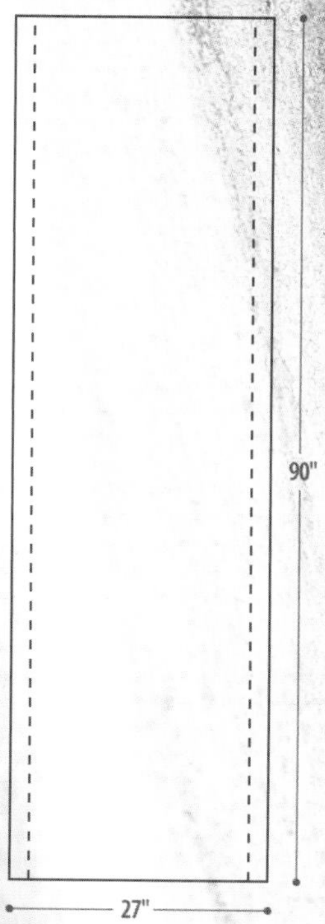

90"

27"

TAHKI Donegal Tweed 5 skeins in 805 (MC); 1 skein each in 803 (C1), 892 (C2), 831 (C3), 845 (C4), 874 (C5), 863 (C6), and 832 (C7)

BIG BANG WRAP

I bought the yarn for this piece in Ireland (although it is available in the US) and began knitting, based on something I had seen there. All the way home on the flight I knit and knit and knit, anxious to see if what I saw in my mind would translate to the fabric. (We knitters can be obsessive, especially when a stitch pattern is both repetitive and interesting.) When done, I was astounded! And others were similarly affected 'cause, when I wear it, it stops traffic! It's one of my favorite pieces, and I gave it the title I did as a way of saying, "Welcome to our universe!"

Pick a dark main color, navy (MC). Now pick 5 brighter contrast colors from one side of the color wheel (CC's). (I chose blue-violet to red-orange.) Now pick 2 CC's complementary to the group. (I chose 2 versions of yellow-green.)

Houndstooth (multiple of 3 sts)
Note Slip all stitches purlwise with yarn to WS (to back on RS rows, to front on WS rows).
Row 1 (RS) With CC indicated in pattern, *k2, sl 1; repeat from* to end.
Row 2 Purl.
Row 3 With MC, *sl 1, k2; repeat from* to end
Row 4 Purl.
Repeat Rows 1–4.

Notes
1 See *Skills-at-a-glance*, page 228, for slip stitch, and bind off in purl. *2* Each 4-row repeat (of Houndstooth and garter ridge) forms a stripe.

WRAP
Lower edging (garter ridge)
With MC, cast on 98 sts.
Knit 2 rows.
  Carry CC's up side until changing CC. Leave all tails 4", and do not weave in.
*With C1, knit 1 row, purl 1 row.
With MC, knit 2 rows.
Repeat from* 4 times more—6 MC ridges and 5 C1 stripes.

Body
Row 1 (RS) With C2, k20, sl 1, place marker (pm), work Row 1 of Slip Stitch across 57 sts, pm, k20.
Row 2 Purl to marker, sl 1, purl to marker, sl 1, p20.
Row 3 With MC, knit to marker, work Row 3 of Slip Stitch to marker, k20.
Row 4 Knit to marker, purl to marker, p1, k20.
Repeat Rows 1–4 while changing colors as follows:
Continue to 2 stripes C2. Cut C2.
Work 3 stripes C3. Cut C3.
Work 5 stripes C4. Cut C4.
Work 2 stripes C5. Cut C5.
Work 3 stripes C6. Cut C6.
Work 5 stripes C7. Cut C7.
Continue to work through colors in sequence and numbers of stripes in 2, 3, 5 sequence.
Work to 120 color stripes—approximately 85".
SHORTEN OR LENGTHEN HERE
  End with 3 color stripes of something.
Upper edging
*With MC, knit 2 rows.
With next color in sequence, knit 1 row then purl 1 row.
Repeat from* 4 times more—5 MC ridges and 5 CC stripes.
With MC, knit 2 rows.
Bind off loosely.

FINISHING
Edging, side without tails
With MC, circular needle, RS facing, and working 1 stitch in from the edge, pick up and knit 1 stitch for every row: 2 sts for each CC stripe and 2 for each garter ridge.
  This is normally too many stitches for the edge, but too many stitches is what makes it flare.
Knit 1 row, purl 1 row, knit 1 row.
Bind off in purl.
To make wrap reversible, sew down edging as invisibly as possible with lengths of MC.
Edging, side with tails
Overhand-knot all pairs of tails. Clip to ¾".
  Because of the extra bulk of the knots, you may choose to pick up and knit only half a stitch from the edge.
Work as for side edging without tails. If needed, work 1 more row of edging to cover the tails.
Block well, stretching side edgings to maximum flare.

EXPerience
- *easy*
- *simple stitch pattern*
- *no finishing*

WRAP
22×58"
RUNNER, MAT
placemat 12×16"
table runner 12×32"
- *without fringe*

10cm/4"

36, 48
18, 26
- *over slip stitch*
- *after blocking*

You'll need

1 2 **3** 4 5 6

- *Light weight*
MC • 660 yds
C1–4 • 80 yds each
MC • 125 yds each mat
CC1–C3 • 25 yds each for each mat
- *Twice as many yds for runner*
- *Something firm and washable*

I used

- *5mm/US9*
- *3.75mm/US5*
60cm/24"

- *4.5mm/G*
- *3.5mm/E*
optional, for crochet cast-on

LINEN-STITCH WRAP

I bought myself a subtly colored and soft-draping woven piece in England and used to drape it over my piano or wear as a shawl. After repeatedly moving it from the piano to my body then back again, I thought "Why don't I just knit one so the piano and I don't have to share?" Linen stitch, knit loosely, seemed the perfect choice.

Choose a dark main color (MC), then 4 contrast colors (CC's), all from one side of the color wheel (see page 9). I chose red (C1)+red-orange (C2)+yellow-orange (C3)+yellow-green (C4).

Linen Stitch (odd number of sts)
Row 1 (RS) With MC or CC as indicated in pattern, and leaving 5" tail, *k1, slip 1 purlwise with yarn to front (sl 1 wyif); repeat from* to last stitch, k1. Cut yarn to 5" tail. Do not turn work; slide stitches to other end of needle.
Row 2 (RS) With MC and leaving 5" tail, *sl 1 wyif, k1; repeat from* to last st, sl 1 wyif. Cut yarn to 5" tail. Do not turn work; slide stitches to other end of needle.
Repeat Rows 1 and 2.

Note
See *Skills-at-a-glance*, page 228, for crochet cast-on and slip stitch.

WRAP
Border
With main color (MC), cast on 251 sts.
I recommend crochet cast-on.
Cut yarn at end of cast-on row to 5" tail. Do not turn work; slide stitches to other end of needle. Work Linen Stitch for 2", using MC for Row 1 and ending with Row 2.
Every inch or so, make overhand knots to finish pairs of tails at edges.
Color pattern
Use contrast colors in Row 1 as follows:
For 3", use C1.

For 2", alternate C1 and C2: *work first Row 1 with C2, next Row 1 with C1; repeat from*, end with C1.
For 3", use C2.
For 2", alternate C3 and C2.
For 3", use C3.
For 2", alternate C4 and C3.
For 3", use C4.
Border
For 2", use MC for Row 1.
Bind off in MC.
Knot all remaining tails, and trim to 4".
Block well.

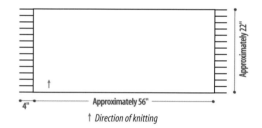

Approximately 22"
Approximately 56"
4"
↑ *Direction of knitting*

GARNSTUDIO Silke-tweed 3 skeins in 06 (MC);
1 skein each in 23 (C1), 13 (C2), 16 (C3), and 14 (C4)

LINEN-STITCH RUNNER AND PLACEMATS

After using the Linen-stitch Wrap over my piano, I thought about knitting something exclusively for home decor. Around that time I replaced my dishes. After a frustrating search for placemats, I thought "Okay, here's my opportunity. Linen stitch knit firmly and in colors of my choosing."

Choose a neutral or a dark color for the main color (MC): I chose off-white, beige, charcoal, or dark violet. Then choose 3 contrast colors from one side of the color wheel: I chose violet (C1), blue-green (C2), and yellow-green (C3) for the neutral version; I chose red-orange (C1), orange (C2), and yellow-green (C3) for the colorful version.

PLACEMAT (RUNNER)

Border

With main color (MC), cast on 103 (205) sts.
  I recommend the crochet cast-on.
Cut yarn at end of cast-on row to 2" tail.
Do not turn work, slide stitches to other end of needle. Work Linen Stitch for 10 rows, using MC for Row 1.
  Every inch or so, make overhand knots to finish pairs of tails at edges.

Color pattern

Use contrast colors (C) in Row 1 as follows:
For 12 rows, use C1.
For 12 rows, alternate C2 and C1: *work first Row 1 with C2, next Row 1 with C1; repeat from*, end with C1.
For 16 rows, use C2.
For 12 rows, alternate C3 and C2.
For 22 rows, use C3.
For 12 rows, alternate C2 and C3.
For 16 rows, use C2.
For 12 rows, alternate C1 and C2.
For 12 rows, use C1.

Border

For 10 rows, use MC for Row 1.
Bind off in MC.
Knot all remaining tails, and trim to 1".
Press well.

Purple placemat, top:
CLASSIC ELITE Provence 1 skein each 2653 (MC), 2658 (C1), 2619 (C2), 2681 (C3).
Other placemats and runner:
CLASSIC ELITE Provence 1 skein 2616 (MC)
SR KERTZER Butterfly Super 10 1 skein 3087 (MC) or 3242 (MC)
CLASSIC ELITE Provence 1 skein each 2649 (C1), 2674 (C2), and 2682 (C3)

12"

1"   ⟵——— 16 (32 for runner)" ———⟶

↑ *Direction of working*

EXPErience
- *easy intermediate*
- *repetitive stitch pattern*
- *simple shaping*
- *simple finishing*

LOOSE FIT

Infant 3 (6, 9, 12) months
A 19 (20, 21, 22)"
B 10 (11, 12, 12)"
C 11½ (12½, 13½, 15)"

10cm/4"

40
24

- *over Tweed Stitch*
- *using larger needles*

You'll need

1 2 **3** 4 5 6

- **Light weight**
MC • 135 (160, 180, 215) yds, solid color
CC • 75 (90, 100, 120) yds, variegated
- **something soft enough for an infant**

I used

- **4mm/US6**
- **3.5mm/US4**

- **Five 19mm/¾"**

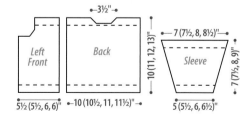

Left Front | Back | Sleeve

←3½"→

10(11, 12, 13)"

7 (7½, 8, 8½)"

7 (7½, 8, 9)"

5½ (5½, 6, 6)" | ←10 (10½, 11, 11½)"→ | 5 (5½, 6, 6½)"

BABY RAINBOW JACKET

I dyed the contrast yarn for this piece in a dye workshop many years ago (an experience I highly recommend). It begged to be knit into a baby sweater—because of the colors and because of the limited amount of yarn. Cheryl Potter, who taught the dye workshop, agreed to replicate my dye job, so something-as-close-as-possible to the original is available to you.

When my son first saw this piece, he said "It looks like a magic eye painting!" And then, because he thinks I'm a genius, he said "Is it?" What a wonderfully imagined thought—that someone could knit a magic eye painting!

Colors chosen are a light, short color change variegated and a main color darker than any in the variegated.

What is normally the wrong side of this stitch pattern is used as the right side for this garment because I think it is prettier and more interesting.

Tweed Stitch (multiple of 2 sts)
Row 1 (WS) With MC, k1, *k1, slip 1 purlwise with yarn in front (sl 1 wyif); repeat from * to last st, k1.
Row 2 (RS) Purl.
Row 3 With CC, k1, *sl 1 wyif, k1, repeat from * to last st, k1.
Row 4 Purl.
Repeat Rows 1–4.

9 months: CHERRY TREE HILL North Country Cotton 1 skein each in Teal Green (MC) and Pastel Rainbow (CC)

Note

See *Skills-at-a-glance*, page 228, for slip stitch and 1-row buttonhole.

BACK

With smaller needles and MC, cast on 56 (58, 60, 64) sts.
Knit 6 rows.
Next row (RS) Knit across, inc 4 sts evenly— 60 (62, 64, 68) sts.
Change to larger needles and begin Tweed Stitch with Row 3.
Work until piece measures to 9 (10, 11, 12)", end with Row 1 or 3.
Cut CC.
SHORTEN OR LENGTHEN HERE
Shape right back neck
Next row (RS) With MC, k22 (23, 24, 26) sts. Put next 16 sts on holder. Turn.
*Bind off 1 st at neck edge, knit to end.
Knit 1 row. Repeat last 2 rows once.
Next RS row Bind off.
Shape left back neck
Return to 22 (23, 24, 26) sts, RS facing.
Knit 2 rows.
Work as Shape right back neck from* to end.

LEFT FRONT

With smaller needles and MC, cast on 31 (31, 33, 35) sts.
Knit 6 rows.
Next row (RS) Knit across, inc 1 st—32 (32, 34, 36) sts.
Change to larger needles and begin Tweed Stitch with Row 3.
Work until piece measures 8 (9, 10, 11)", end with Row 2 or 4.
Shape neck
Continue Tweed Stitch through shaping.
Bind off at neck edge 5 sts once, 2 sts twice, 1 st 3 times—20 (20, 22, 24) sts, end with Row 1 or 3.
Cut CC.
With MC, knit 6 rows.
Bind off.

RIGHT FRONT

Work as Left Front but with reverse shaping.
This means you will Shape neck on RS rows.

SLEEVES

With smaller needles and MC, cast on 26 (28, 30, 34) sts.
Knit 6 rows.

Next row (RS) Knit across, inc 6 sts evenly—32 (34, 36, 40) sts.
Change to larger needles and begin Tweed Stitch with Row 3.
Work 4 rows more.
Inc row (RS) P1, work lifted inc in next st (inc 1, see page 115), work to last 2 sts, inc 1, p1.
Repeat Inc row every 8 rows 4 times more—42 (44, 46, 50) sts.
Work even to 6 (6½, 7, 8)" from beginning, end with Row 1 or 3. Cut CC.
SHORTEN OR LENGTHEN HERE
With MC, knit 6 rows.
Bind off.

FINISHING

Sew shoulder seams.
Neck edging
With RS facing, MC, and smaller needle, pick up and knit around neck edge as follows:
  • 1 st for every bound-off st and 1 st for every 2-row step between bound-off sts at Front neck shaping;
  • 1 st for every MC garter ridge on either side of shoulders;
  • 1 st for every st on holder at center Back neck.
Knit 2 rows, then bind off.
Button band
  Decide which side you want for the buttons—left for female, right for male.
With RS facing, MC and smaller needles, pick up and k 1 st for every 2 rows along Front edge.
Knit 5 rows, then bind off.
Mark places on this edging for 5 buttons. Mark other Front to correspond.
Buttonhole band
With RS facing, MC, and smaller needles, pick up and k 1 st for every 2 rows along Front edge.
Next row (WS) Knit.
Make buttonholes: *Next row* (RS) Knit, AT SAME TIME work a 2-st, 1-row buttonhole at each marker.
Knit 3 rows.
Bind off.
Sew buttons to match placement of buttonholes.
Sew Sleeves to garment, matching center of Sleeves with shoulder seams.
Sew Sleeve and side seams.

EXPErience

- *easy intermediate*
- *repetitive stitch pattern*
- *simple shaping*
- *simple finishing*

OVERSIZED FIT

Man's S (M, L, 1X, 2X)

A 41 (45, 49, 53, 57)"

B 26 (26½, 27, 27½, 28)"

C 31 (31½, 32, 32½, 33)"

10cm/4"

32

16

- *over Tweed Stitch*
- *using larger needle*
- *after blocking*

You'll need

1 2 3 **4** 5 6

- *Medium weight*

MC • 680 (765, 850, 930, 1025) yds, solid color

CC• 475 (535, 590, 650, 715) yds, variegated

I used

- *5mm/US8*
- *4.5mm/US7*

SLIP-INTO-COLOR PULLOVER

I love this stitch pattern, known as tweed (or half-linen) stitch. (I used it extensively on my first book, *Styles,* a book on using up leftovers in knitting, and it is explored in the plaid garments of this book.) Here it is shown in a simple incarnation: 2 rows main color (MC), 2 rows contrast color (CC), and the variegated contrast yarn does all the color work for you.

The colors used here are a dark neutral plus a brighter, long-color-change variegated. (A shorter-color-change variegated would work just as well.) Do make sure that the color of the background yarn never appears in the variegated.

The garment is over-sized but slimming because of the side panels added later. If you want a slimmer fit, make narrower side panels.

I like what is normally considered the wrong side of this stitch pattern shown on the public side. It's just more interesting.

Tweed stitch (multiple of 2 sts)

Row 1 (WS) With MC, k1, *k1, sl 1 purlwise with yarn to front (sl 1 wyif), repeat from* to last st, k1.

Row 2 Purl.

Row 3 With CC, k1, *sl 1 wyif, k1, repeat from* to last st, k1.

Row 4 Purl.

Repeat Rows 1–4.

Note

See *Skills-at-a-glance*, page 228, for slip stitch and 3-needle bind-off.

BACK

With smaller needles and MC, cast on 66 (72, 80, 88, 96) sts.

Knit 10 rows.

Next row (RS) Knit across, increase evenly 6 (8, 8, 8, 8) sts—72 (80, 88, 96, 104) sts.

Change to larger needles and begin Tweed Stitch with Row 3.

Work even until piece measures 25 (25½, 26, 26½, 27)", end with Row 1 or 3.

SHORTEN OR LENGTHEN HERE

Cut CC. With MC, knit 4 rows.

Shape right back neck

Next row (RS) With MC, k24 (28, 32, 36, 40).

Put next 24 sts on holder. Turn.

*Bind off 1 st at neck edge, knit to end.

Knit 1 row.

Repeat last 2 rows once.

Next RS row Bind off.

Shape left back neck

Return to 24 (28, 32, 36, 40) sts, RS facing.

With MC, knit 2 rows.

Work as right back neck from* to end.

FRONT

I made no effort to make this variegated yarn match at the sides. MC panels (added later) interrupt the colors.

Work as Back until piece measures 23 (23½, 24, 24½, 25)", end with Row 1 or 3.

Shape left front neck

Continue in Tweed Stitch until directed otherwise.

Next row (RS) Work 29 (33, 37, 41, 45) sts. Put next 14 sts on holder. Turn.

*Bind off at neck edge 2 sts once, then 1 st 5 times—22 (26, 30, 34, 38) sts.

End with Row 1 or 3.

Cut CC. With MC, knit 10 rows.

Bind off.

Shape right front neck

Return to 29 (33, 37, 41, 45) sts, RS facing.

Work 2 rows Tweed Stitch.

Work as left front neck from* to end.

Man's XL: BROWN SHEEP Lamb's Pride 5 skeins in M-150 (MC), NORO Kureyon 6 balls in 52 (CC)

SLEEVES

With smaller needles and MC, cast on 34 (36, 38, 40, 42) sts.
Knit 10 rows.

Next row (RS) Knit across, inc 10 (10, 12, 14, 16) sts evenly—
44, (46, 50, 54, 58) sts.

Change to larger needles, begin Tweed Stitch with Row 3 and
work 2 rows.

Inc row (RS) P1, work lifted inc in next st (inc 1, see page 115),
work to last 2 sts, inc 1, p1.

Repeat Inc row every 4 rows 14 (17, 19, 21, 23) times more—74
(82, 90, 98, 106) sts.

Work even until Sleeve measures 21 (20½, 20, 19½, 19)", end
with a WS row.

SHORTEN OR LENGTHEN HERE

Cut CC. With MC, knit 10 rows.

Bind off.

FINISHING

*If you agree that the purl side of Tweed Stitch is more
interesting, make it the RS and proceed with finishing.*

Sew right shoulder seam.

Neck edging

With RS facing, begin at left Front neck with MC and smaller
needle, pick up and knit around neck edge as follows:

- 1 st for every MC garter ridge;
- 1 st for every bound-off st and 1 st for every 2-row
  step between bound-off sts at all neck shaping;
- 1 st for every st on holder.

Knit 7 more rows, then bind off.

Sew left shoulder seam and neck edging.

Assembly

Sew Sleeves to garment, matching center of Sleeves with
shoulder seams.

I used the ratio of 1 st to 2 rows.

Side panels

Do this on all 4 sides, from bottom of Sleeve to lower edges of
Front or Back.

With RS facing, MC and smaller needles, pick up and knit 1 st
for every 2 rows down side.

Knit 9 more rows. Leave stitches on needle.

When adjacent side is done, put RS of Front and Back together,
then 3-needle bind-off to finish side seams.

Sew Sleeve seams.

**Top photo shows Rows 1 and 3 of Tweed Stitch facing, bottom photo
shows Rows 2 and 4 facing.**

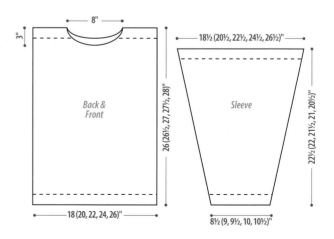

Woman's M: GARNSTUDIO Karisma Superwash
7 balls in 53 (MC), KOIGU Kersti 5 balls in K104 (CC)
Man's L: LANA GROSSA Due Chine 12 balls in 402 (MC),
10 balls in 407 (CC)

EXPErience

- *easy intermediate*
- *simple stitch pattern*
- *simple shaping*

LOOSE FIT

Woman's S (M, L, 1X, 2X)
A 38 (42, 45½, 49½, 55)"
B 20½ (21, 21½, 22, 22½)"
C 29 (29½, 30, 30½, 31)"
Man's S (M, L, 1X, 2X)
A 41½ (44½, 47½, 53, 56)"
B 26 (26½, 27, 27½, 28)"
C 31½ (32, 32½, 33, 33½)"

Woman's, Man's
10cm/4 "

30, 19
17, 11

- *over Faux Check*
- *using larger needles*
- *after blocking*

You'll need

3 OR **5**

- *Light weight*
MC • **690 (800, 880, 990, 1120) yds**
CC • **640 (740, 815, 910, 1040) yds**
- *Bulky weight*
MC • **640 (700, 730, 825, 890) yds**
CC • **565 (615, 640, 730, 795) yds**

I used

- *4mm/US6*
- *6mm/US10*

- *3.5mm/US4*
- *5mm/US8*
50cm/20"

FAUX CHECK PULLOVER

Here is something called Lampshade stitch worked more-or-less as I originally saw it. But here it's done over 4 rows rather than 8. So while the original resembled a lampshade, this looks more like a houndstooth check. I love its appearance of vertical stripes, produced from knitting an easy horizontal pattern.

Because the main color (MC) in each is a very undemanding gray, I used somewhat demanding contrast colors (CC)—a warm orange or a bright variegated.

This stitch pattern can be knit to a looser gauge than the yarn weight suggests and still produce an appropriate fabric. Two gauges are given here. For the woman's garment a Light-weight yarn is knit to a 17-st (Medium-weight) gauge; for the man's, a Bulky-weight yarn is knit to an 11-st (Super Bulky-weight) gauge.

3×1 Rib (multiple of 4 sts+3)
RS rows *K3, p1; repeat from* to last 3 sts, k3.
WS rows *P3, k1; repeat from* to last 3 sts, p3.

1×1 Rib (multiple of 2 sts+3)
RS rows K2, *p1, k1; repeat from* to last st, k1.
WS rows P2, *k1, p1; repeat from* to last st, p1.

Faux Check (multiple of 4 sts + 3)

Row 1 (RS) With CC, *k3, [knit into stitch 2 rows below (see page 114), knit next stitch, pass 'dipped' stitch over: 1 dip st made]; repeat from* to last 3 sts, k3.
Row 2 Purl.
Row 3 With MC, k1, *make 1 dip st, k3; repeat from* to last 2 sts, make 1 dip st, k1.
Row 4 Purl.
Repeat Rows 1–4.

Note

See *Skills-at-a-glance*, page 228, for grafting and bind off in pattern.

FRONT / BACK (MAKE 2)

With smaller needles and MC, cast on 83 (91, 99, 107, 119) or 59 (63, 67, 75, 79) sts.
Work 3 × 1 Rib or 1 × 1 Rib to 1", end with a WS row.
Knit 1 row, purl 1 row.
Begin with Row 1 of Faux Check, and work until piece measures 17 (17½, 18, 18½, 19)" or 23 (23½, 24, 24½, 25)", end with Row 2 or 4.
SHORTEN OR LENGTHEN HERE
Bind off.

LEFT SLEEVE

With smaller needles and MC, cast on 39 (39, 43, 47, 51) sts or 27 (27, 27, 31, 31) sts.
Work Rib to 3", end with a WS row.
Knit 1 row, purl 1 row.
  Continue Faux Check through all shaping that follows. You will always make dip stitches over dip stitches.
Work Rows 1–4 of Faux Check.
Inc row P1, work lifted inc in next st (see page 115), work to last 2 sts, inc 1, p1.
Repeat Inc row every 4 rows 19 (23, 25, 27, 27) or 13 (15, 17, 17, 19) times more—79 (87, 95, 103, 107) or 55 (59, 63, 67, 71) sts.
Work even until Sleeve measures 19½ (19, 18½, 18, 17)" or 21 (21, 20½, 19½, 19½)".
SHORTEN OR LENGTHEN HERE
Shape Saddle

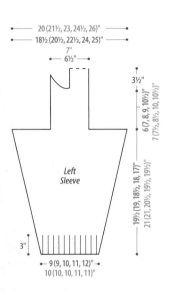

20 (21½, 23, 24½, 26)"
18½ (20½, 22½, 24, 25)"
7"
6½"
3½"
6 (7, 8, 9, 10½)"
7 (7½, 8½, 10, 10½)"

Left Sleeve

19½ (19, 18½, 18, 17)"
21 (21, 20½, 19½, 19½)"

3"

9 (9, 10, 11, 12)"
10 (10, 10, 11, 11)"

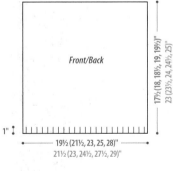

Front/Back

17½ (18, 18½, 19, 19½)"
23 (23½, 24, 24½, 25)"

1"

19½ (21½, 23, 25, 28)"
21½ (23, 24½, 27½, 29)"

Bind off at beginning of next 2 rows 26 (30, 34, 38, 40) or 18 (20, 22, 24, 26) sts—27 or 19 sts.
Work even until saddle measures 6 (7, 8, 9, 10½)" or 7 (7½, 8½, 10, 10½)", end with a RS row.

Shape front neck

Next row (WS) Work 14 or 10 sts. Turn, leaving 13 or 9 sts for back neck.
Bind off 4 or 3 sts at beginning of RS row.
Work WS rows even while shaping neck as follows:
At beginning of RS rows, bind off 3 sts once, 2 sts once, 1 st twice, 3 sts once or 2 sts once, 1 st twice, 3 sts once.

Back neck shaping

Return to remaining sts, WS facing.
Bind off 1 st at beginning of next 2 WS rows, then work even until back neck measures 3½".
Put sts on holder.

RIGHT SLEEVE

Work as Left Sleeve but reverse shaping by binding off at front neck on WS rows and at back neck on RS rows.

FINISHING

Match upper corners of Back to corner of Sleeves (at bind off).
Sew Sleeve saddles across upper Back, and sew Sleeve bind-off edge to Back, seaming 3 sts for every 5 rows.
Add or subtract rows of back saddles so live sts meet at center Back, graft live sts together.
  If you don't like your grafting, pull grafting thread tight to form seam with no seam allowance.
Sew Sleeves to Front in same manner.
  Saddles will end approximately 2" from center Front.
Sew Sleeve and side seams.
Neck edging

With MC and smaller circular needle, begin at center back neck to pick up and knit as follows:
• 2 sts for every 3 rows across back;
• 1 st for every bound-off st plus 1 st for every 2-row step between bound-off sts at all neck shaping;
• 1 st for every bound-off st at open space of center Front.
Count the number of sts, and decrease if necessary to a multiple of 4 or 2.
Work 3 × 1 Rib or 1 × 1 Rib for 1".
Bind off in pattern.

LITTLE SQUARES

EXPerience

- *easy*
- *simple stitch pattern*
- *simple shaping*
- *simple finishing*

OVERSIZED FIT

Woman's S-M (L-1X, 2X+)
A 60 (66, 70)"
B 24"
C 30"

10cm/4"

25

13½

- *over Little Squares*
- *after blocking*
- *using larger needles*

1 2 3 **4** 5 6

- *Medium weight*
MC • 1120 (1200, 1280) yds
CC • 680 (730, 780) yds
- *variegated mohair (MC)*
- *variegated ribbon (CC)*

I used

- *5mm/US8*
- *4mm/US6*

- *4mm/G*

Here the lampshade stitch pattern is worked not at all as it was originally shown. Yes, 2 colors are used, but only one does the 'dip,' the one doing the dipping is knit back rather than purled, and the wrong side is worn publicly.

I love how this looks in 2 luxury yarns—mohair as the main color (MC) and ribbon as the contrast (CC). But this can be done with virtually anything—contrasting or coordinating, luxury or not.

The yarns used have a common tint of red-violet, but the ribbon goes to orange and yellow-orange, and the mohair goes to green and blue-green. The combination illustrates a triad (see page 11), but it's also an example of related variegateds and integration.

The yarns used are actually one category finer than the gauge offered: medium yarns are knit to a bulky gauge. It's the nature of this stitch pattern that it can be knit to a looser gauge to produce an appropriate fabric.

1 × 1 Rib (multiple of 2 sts + 3)
RS rows K2, *p1, k1; repeat from*
to last st, k1.
WS rows P2, *k1, p1; repeat from* to last st, p1.

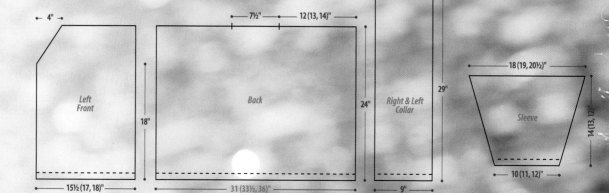

S–M: ARTFUL YARNS Portrait 7 balls in 112 (MC),
Celebrity 7 balls in 37 (C)

Little Squares (multiple of 4 sts + 5)
Rows 1, 3 (WS) With MC, knit.
Rows 2, 4 Purl.
Row 5 (WS) With CC, k4, * [knit into stitch 4 rows below (see page 114), knit next stitch, pass 'dipped' st over], k3; repeat from * to last st, k1;
Row 6 Knit.
Repeat Rows 1–6.

Note
See *Skills-at-a-glance*, page 228, for SSK, k2tog, kf&b, bind off in purl, and eyelet buttonhole.

BACK
With smaller needles and MC, cast on 105 (113, 121) sts.
Work 1 × 1 rib for 1", end with a RS row.
Change to larger needles. Work Little Squares until piece measures approximately 24", end with Row 6.
SHORTEN OR LENGTHEN HERE
Bind off in CC and in purl.

LEFT FRONT
With smaller needles and MC, cast on 53 (57, 61) sts.
Work as for Back until piece measures 18", end with Row 2, 4, or 6.
V-neck shaping
Dec row (WS) K1, SSK, work to end.
Repeat Dec row every WS row 12 times more—40 (44, 48) sts.
  Maintain stitch pat, but do not work a dip in the first 3 sts of any row.
Work even to same length as Back, then bind off in purl.

RIGHT FRONT
Work as Left Front but with reverse shaping.
  Do not make a dip in the last 3 sts of any row, and decrease as follows: (WS) work to last 3 sts, k2tog, k1.

SLEEVES
With smaller needles and MC, cast on 33 (37, 41) sts.
Work 1 × 1 rib for 1", end with a RS row.
Change to larger needles.
Work Little Squares, Rows 1–5.
Inc row (RS) K1, kf&b, work in Little Squares to last 2 sts, kf&b, k1.
  Maintain the stitch pat through shaping.
Repeat Inc row every 4th row 13 times more—61 (65, 69) sts.

Work even until Sleeve measures approximately 14 (13, 12)", end with Row 6.
SHORTEN OR LENGTHEN HERE
Bind off in CC and in purl.

RIGHT COLLAR
With smaller needles and MC, cast on 29 sts.
Work as for Back until piece measures approximately 29", end with Row 5.
  Don't worry about the ribbon carried up the side; that will be covered later with a crocheted trim.
SHORTEN OR LENGTHEN HERE
  Piece should be 5" longer than Back.
Put stitches on holder.

LEFT COLLAR
Work as for Right Collar until piece measures approximately 10", end with Row 6.
Make eyelet buttonhole, next row K13, k2tog, yo, work to end.
Work until piece measures approximately 13", end with Row 6.
Make second eyelet buttonhole.
Work to same length as Right Collar, end with Row 4.
Put stitches on holder.

FINISHING
Sew shoulder seams.
Graft live sts of Collars together (in garter stitch, see page 46).
With RS of Fronts facing and WS of Collar facing, sew Collar to Fronts, easing extra length at neck corners and across center Back.
  Remember that the bumpier side of the MC is the RS.
With crochet hook, CC, and RS facing, crochet along outside edge of Collar as follows: working loosely, make 1 sc (page 44) in every row of MC, 1 sc in every ridge of CC.
Sew Sleeves to sides of garment, matching center of Sleeves to shoulder seams.
Sew side and Sleeve seams.
Sew buttons to WS of Right Collar to match placement of buttonholes.
Block garment (by washing), stretching center Back to extra length while still damp.
  This stretching will help the center back hang straighter. Because it is a very simple and unshaped garment, the center back will tend to hike up.

EXPErience
- *easy intermediate*
- *simple stitch pattern*
- *simple shaping*

LOOSE FIT

Man's *S (M, L, 1X, 2X)*

A *41 (45½, 48, 52½, 57½)"*

B *(Front) 23 (23½, 24, 24½, 25)"*

(Back is 3" longer)

C *32½ (33, 33½, 34, 34½)"*

10cm/4"

22

13½

- *over Lampshade stitch*
- *using larger needles*
- *after blocking*

You'll need

1 2 3 **4** 5 6

- *Medium weight*
C1, C2 • 555 (630, 680, 775, 860) yds each

I used

- *5mm/US8*

- *4mm/US6, 60cm/24" long*

WRONG-SIDE SWEATER

Lampshade stitch is a wonderful example of 'stripes that aren't,' and I've played with it through this chapter. Here the stitch pattern is written as the original, but the colors are not highly contrasting. And again, I turned the fabric inside out. The result is still simple to knit, but the subtly-colored fabric is very different from the other versions. It's fun to learn a stitch pattern and then alter it!

Colors chosen were slightly-variegated shades of 2 analogous colors: red-violet + red-orange.

This garment could be made for a woman. Just drop down one size (a woman's M equals a man's S), and make it the length you wish (with the sleeves 4" shorter for someone 5'4").

The row gauge is highly affected by blocking, so block before taking measurements. Also, I found that the garment stretched over the shoulders, so the sleeves are knit to 1½" shorter than the finished C measurement suggests.

This stitch pattern can be knit to a looser gauge than the yarn weight suggests. Here, a medium weight yarn is knit to a bulky gauge.

2×2 Rib in rows (multiple of 4 sts + 2)
Row 1 (RS) *K2, p2; repeat from*, end k2.
Row 2 *P2, k2; repeat from*, end p2.
Repeat Rows 1 and 2.

2×2 Rib in rounds
All Rnds *K2, p2; repeat from*.

Lampshade Stitch (multiple of 4 sts + 3)
Row 1 (WS) With C1, p1, k2, * [knit into stitch 4 rows below (see page 114), knit next stitch, pass 'dipped' st over; 1 dip made], k3; repeat from* to last 4 sts, make 1 dip, k2, p1.

Rows 2, 4, 6, 8 Using same yarn as previous row, k3, purl to last 3 sts, k3.
Row 3 With C1, p1, knit to last st, p1.
Row 5 With C2, p1, k4, *make 1 dip, k3; repeat from* to last 6 sts, make 1 dip, k4, p1.
Row 7 With C2, p1, knit to last st, p1.
Repeat Rows 1–8.

Note
See *Skills-at-a-glance*, page 228, for SSK, k2tog, SSP, p2tog, lifted inc, grafting, and bind off in knit and purl.

FRONT
With smaller needles and C1, cast on 70 (78, 82, 90, 98) sts.
Work 2 × 2 Rib for 5 rows.
Change to larger needles and C2.
  Carry yarn not in use up side.
Next row (WS) P1, knit across but inc 1 in center of row, purl last st—71 (79, 83, 91, 99) sts.
Begin Lampshade stitch with Row 6 (in C2), and work even until piece measures 17 (17½, 18, 18½, 19)", end with Row 2 or 6.
  Block to get an accurate measurement.
SHORTEN OR LENGTHEN HERE
Bind off in knit.

BACK
Make as Front but 16 rows longer.

LEFT SLEEVE
With smaller needles and C1, cast on 30 (30, 34, 34, 38) sts.
Work as for Front through first Row 2 (2, 8, 8, 8) of Lampshade stitch—31 (31, 35, 35, 39) sts.
Continue stitch pat through all shaping that follows. Keep p1 & k2 at beginning and end of all WS rows and k3 at beginning and end of all RS rows.
Inc row K3, work lifted inc in next purl st (page 115), work to last 4 sts, inc 1, k3.
Repeat Inc row every 6 (6, 4, 4, 4) rows 14 (14, 16, 16, 18) times more—61 (61, 69, 69, 77) sts.
Work even until Sleeve measures 20½ (20, 20, 19½, 18½)", end with Row 2 or 6.
  Block before measuring.
SHORTEN OR LENGTHEN HERE
Shape saddle
  Maintain stitch pat through all shaping.

At beginning of next 2 rows, bind off 9 (9, 13, 13, 17) sts—43 sts.
Work even until saddle measures 7 (8¼, 8¾, 10, 11¼)", end with a WS row.
Shape front V-neck
Next row (RS) Work 21 sts (back neck), bind off 2 sts, work to end—20 front-neck sts remain.
Working over front-neck sts only, bind off 2 sts at beginning of next 10 RS rows.
Shape back neck
Return to 21 sts, WS facing.
Bind off 1 st at beginning of next 2 WS rows.
Work even in Lampshade Stitch until back neck measures 3½".
Put stitches on holder.

RIGHT SLEEVE
Work as Left Sleeve but reverse neck shaping by binding off on WS rather than RS rows, and vice versa.

FINISHING
Match upper corners of Back to corner of Sleeves (at bind off).
Sew Sleeve saddles across upper Back and sew Sleeve bind-off to sides of Back, seaming 3 sts for every 5 rows.
Add or subtract rows of back saddles so live sts meet at center back: graft live sts together.
  If you don't like your grafting, pull grafting thread tight to form seam with no seam allowance.
Sew Sleeves to Front in same manner.
  Don't worry if saddles don't meet at center front; if there is a space remaining, the neck edging will fill it.
Sew Sleeve and side seams, leaving side seams open 4" at lower edges.
  The Back is 3" longer than the Front: if you don't leave the side open above the point where the Front ends, this will look like a mistake!
Neck edging
With C1 or C2 (whichever you prefer) and circular needle, begin at right shoulder to pick up and knit as follows:
  • 5 sts at back neck shaping;
  • 2 sts for every 3 rows across unshaped back neck;
  • 3 sts for every 2-st bind-off along V-neck shaping;
  • any number sts necessary to close space (if there is one) at center front neck.
Next rnd Work 2 × 2 Rib to center front, but k2 at center front.
  It doesn't matter what precedes the k2. Whatever you did before it, do immediately after also.

Continue 2 × 2 Rib to center back.

If necessary decrease as you approach right shoulder, so round ends with 4-st repeat.

Miter rnd Work rib to 2 sts before k2 at center front, SSK (or SSP), k2 at center, k2tog (or p2tog), work to end.

You decide which decrease looks best.

Next rnd Work even.

Repeat last 2 rnds once more.

Next row Bind off in pattern, AT SAME TIME repeat miter at center front.

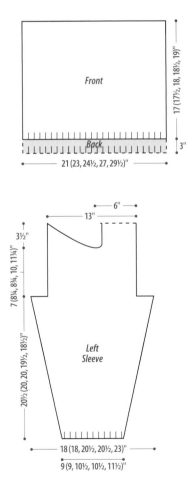

Front

17 (17½, 18, 18½, 19)"

Back

3"

21 (23, 24½, 27, 29½)"

6"

13"

3½"

7 (8¼, 8¾, 10, 11¾)"

Left
Sleeve

20½ (20, 20, 19½, 18½)"

18 (18, 20½, 20½, 23)"

9 (9, 10½, 10½, 11½)"

L: MANOS DEL URUGUAY
100% Wool 5 skeins each 100 (C1) and 104 (C2)

- *intermediate*
- *repetitive stitch pattern*
- *mid-level shaping*

Finished measurements
Width (at base) 3½"
Length 60"

10cm/4"

40 ▦
26
- *over Linen Stitch*

1 2 **3** 4 5 6

- *Light weight*
C1–3 • 30 yds each

I used

- *4mm/US6*

- *3.5mm/E*
for crochet cast-on

ED'S TIE

For years I have been hosted by my friend, Ed Jernigan, to speak to a group of high school students on a summer enrichment experience, the Shad Valley Programme. After some years of this, he decided the students needed more than my Creativity lecture; they needed to learn to knit!

The first year I was practically the only knitter in the room of 45 students and 5 staff. But from the beginning, staff and students were addicted. Now with each new crop of students we 'addict,' the staff—including the director, my friend Ed—helps demonstrate. We've now brought over 100 new knitters into the fold, and the guys are every bit as enthusiastic as the girls.

The first year Ed learned to knit, he made himself a tie: in garter stitch, out of dish-cloth cotton. Ed deserves a second tie to add to his collection, so I offer this. In fact, shouldn't all those wonderful guys who knit have something colorful but simple to make and wear?

Choose 3 colors: 2 neutrals plus one stronger color. In these examples, I used pale beige and taupe with turquoise or dark brown and grey with denim blue.

The length of this tie will accommodate a half-Windsor knot.

Linen Stitch A (over an odd number of sts)
Note Slip all stitches as if to purl.
RS rows *K1, slip 1 with yarn in front (sl 1 wyif); repeat from* to last st, k1.
WS rows Sl 1 wyif, *p1, sl 1 with yarn in back (sl 1 wyib); repeat from* to last 2 sts, p1, sl 1 wyif.

Linen Stitch B (over an odd number of sts)
RS rows (RS) K2, *sl 1 wyif, k1; repeat from* to last st, k1.
WS rows Sl 1 wyif, *sl 1 wyib, p1; repeat from* to last 2 sts, sl 1 wyib, sl 1 wyif.

Note

See *Skills-at-a-glance*, page 228, for crochet cast-on, slip stitch, SSK, k2tog, and p2tog.

TIE

With C1, cast on 23 sts.

I recommend the crochet cast-on.

Work Linen Stitch A (pat A) as follows:

With C2, work RS Row.

With C3, work WS Row.

With C1, work RS Row.

With C2, work WS Row.

Continue with pat A, working 1 row in each color (see page 42) and in C1, C2, C3 sequence until tie measures 5", end with WS Row.

It is absolutely essential to slip the first and last st of every WS row. Failure to do this will ruin the edges of the tie.

A dec row (RS) K1, SSK, *sl 1 wyif, k1; repeat from* to last 4 sts, sl 1 wyif, k2tog, k1—21 sts.

Beginning with WS Row, work pat B in color sequence.

Work pat B, until tie measures 10", end with a WS row.

As you continue to shape the tie, it can be difficult to remember where you are in the stitch pattern. If you have 23, 19, 15, or 11 sts on your needle, you are working pat A. If you have 21, 17, or 13 sts on your needle, you are working pat B.

Set-up for B dec row (RS) K1, sl next 2 sts wyif, *k1, sl 1 wyif; repeat from* to last 4 sts, k1, sl next 2 sts wyif, k1.

B dec row Sl 1 wyif, p 2 sl sts tog, *sl 1 wyib, p1; repeat from* to last 4 sts, sl 1 wyib, p 2 sl sts tog, sl 1 wyif—19 sts.

Work pat A until tie measures 15", end with a WS row.

Work A dec row—17 sts.

Work pat B until tie measures 20", end with a WS row.

Work Set up for B dec row and B dec row—15 sts.

Work pat A until tie measures 23", end with a WS row.

Work A dec row—13 sts.

Work pat B until tie measures 26", end with a WS row.

Work Set-up row for B and B dec row—11 sts.

Work pat A over remaining 11 sts until tie measures 58". Press tie well before trying on.

With pressing and tying, it stretches to 60".

LENGTHEN HERE

Bind off.

Dark tie: ELSEBETH LAVOLD Silky Tweed 1 ball each in 7, 4, and 3

Light tie: ELSEBETH LAVOLD Cotton Patine 1 ball each in 002, 003, 008

1½"

32"

58"

3"

3"

5"

5"

5"

5"

←—3½"—→

The dip technique

Check out rescue techniques for common color mistakes in Oops, pages 224-225.

This is a way of producing a stitch by working into a stitch somewhere below. It's an easy way of knitting stripes that do not end up looking like stripes. And I believe it has innumerable possibilities of usage, only some of which are introduced in this chapter.

It is with tongue-in-cheek that I call this the 'dip' stitch. But it does aptly describe the technique with which it is made. And I don't know that it has any other official name? I learned it as a part of a stitch pattern called 'lampshade stitch,' and I think I have heard it called 'flame' stitch. But there are many ways to use it that don't look like lampshades or flames, so I thought it best to give it this more descriptive name.

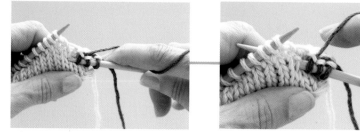 

1 After knitting the number of stitches indicated by the stitch pattern (here I show 3 already knit), insert right needle into stitch below stitch on left needle. (The pattern will tell you how many rows below; here I show 4).

2 Make a stitch as usual, drawing a long enough loop to not distort the fabric.

3 Now knit the stitch on the left needle as usual.

4 Pass the dip stitch over the just-knit stitch (1 dip made).

This photo shows some of the next dip row.

Lifted increase in purl

Sometimes a stitch pattern is simplified if increases are made on the purl side.

The simple 'Make 1' (M1) increase can also be made on the wrong side. Just work as you would on the right side, but purl rather than knit.

On a purl side and after working one or more selvedge stitches,

1 insert right needle as if to purl into purl bump below next stitch on left needle,

2 Purl into bump as usual.

3 Now purl next stitch on left needle as usual.
Work to selvedge stitch(es) + 1 stitch remaining on left needle.
Repeat Steps 1–3.

Here is the result as seen from the right side.

Waste yarn

Sometimes we do a temporary bind-off. Why? Sometimes you don't have enough holders to hold the live stitches left behind by the pattern. Sometimes so many holders would be required that they would weigh down the knitting. And sometimes putting stitches on a thread is more work than just knitting and binding off. But you don't want to waste good yarn to bind off, so use scrap yarn—commonly referred to as 'waste' yarn.

TEMPORARY OR PROVISIONAL CAST ON
Waste yarn can often be used for the temporary cast-on of a piece. This cast-on would then be removed to work down from 'live' stitches. The best cast-on method to use (because it can be ripped out so easily) is the crochet cast-on. See *Skills At-a -Glance*, page 228.

HOW KNITTING CAN CHANGE THE WORLD

There is a Ben Harper song that runs through my head: "you can change the world, with your own two hands/make a better place, with your own two hands/make a kinder place, with your own two hands." I like to think he'd approve of what follows.

One way to think of creativity is using our hands to create something that did not exist before and that adds value to our world. Even if we leave it at this rather limited definition, what you are doing—working with your hands and inspiring others to do so—does this. Maria Montessori said the following:

> All men will resemble one another in the way they use their feet. But no-one can tell what any given man will do with his hands.... The hand is the direct connect with man's soul... and in the light of history we see it connected with the development of civilization.... If men had only used speech to communicate their thought, no traces would remain of past generations.

This is pretty important stuff: you take time to work with your hands, you give this work value, you inspire others to do the same, and civilization is enriched.

But I would argue a more profound definition of creativity, one that digs deeper and resonates with some pretty great thinkers who saw creativity differently—as simply problem solving. From this place, we need creativity even more. Our problems haven't diminished; they've multiplied and become more threatening. Our world needs creative thinkers.

How is creativity taught? The great thinkers I have read say that it cannot be taught. It does happen, though. And for it to happen, the following factors need to be present:
- an environment in which creativity is supported and valued;
- exposure to (good) role models;
- access to materials;
- the opportunity for persistent practice.

Isn't this your home when you knit—when you provide an environment in which it's okay to work with your hands, learn a new skill, solve problems as you develop your craft? It does not matter what the result is. (You did notice that there was no mention of 'product' in the factors list?) It's the attempt and the practice and the environment and the role-modeling that matter.

Of course, like me, you will sometimes struggle a little too much and find yourself providing yet another kind of role model. One of our children went off to university and called at the end of the first month to say, "I was in the common room the other night, working hard. Behind me was someone swearing like crazy, so I turned around to see who was knitting!"

So sometimes our problems carry us to a place we wish they would not. But that's okay. We must continue. Because in doing so, we provide an environment in which the struggle to learn and accomplish is seen as a good thing. In simply doing this, we intersect the factors essential for creativity, and we provide an invaluable service to those around us, because this is how their creativity is fostered. In simply doing this, we could affect and inspire someone to take on the problems of the world, to change the world, to make it a better place for us all. Makes a day worth living, dontcha think?

THE KNITTING EXPERIENCE

THE 2-COLOR TRADITION

We immediately recognize the knitting of this chapter as a beautiful and much-loved knitting style: 2 colors across a row, alternating in some sort of motif. Have you ever considered the many places from which it originates and the many ways in which it is expressed?

An entire garment can be worked in 2 starkly contrasting colors, in a few bright colors, or in many softly graded colors; the motif can be a single large one, a few middle-sized ones, or innumerable tiny ones; these motifs can be intricate and figurative or as simple as X's and O's. All of these possibilities are expressed in the traditions of the Scandinavian countries, the British Isles, and of South America.

So what do we call this technique? What term can we use that encompasses all traditions? Machine knitters may refer to this knitting as 'fairisle'—one word, no caps. While it's convenient to do so, you will get an argument from traditional knitters. The Fair Isles are certainly not the only place the tradition developed, and the Fair Isle tradition has its own very particular expression of this technique.

How to refer to this style of knitting? There really is no single word for it. You might have heard it called '2-color stranded' or '2-color circular.' These kinda sorta work. Sometimes 2 colors are stranded in a garment...but sometimes they are woven. Mostly it is 2 colors at a time...but sometimes more are carried. Mostly it is knit in the round (rather than back and forth in rows...but sometimes not.

Please forgive me for not finding one succinct and inclusive title for this chapter. Many have tried and failed: I simply join them. Let us just conclude that it's a tribute to the tradition that it cannot be easily summarized.

There is much here to be explored. I do not pretend to do anything but scratch the surface, give choices for the mastery of this technique, offer simple garments on which to hone your skills, and hope to whet your appetite for a truly, richly, gorgeous expression of our craft.

Chapter Four

The Patterns

Additional Skills

EXPerience

- *easy*
- *easy stitch/ color pattern*
- *no shaping*
- *simple finishing*

One size
pre-fulling:
A *(circumference) 32"*
B *(height) 16"*
post-fulling:
A *(circumference) 25"*
B *(height) 12"*

10cm/4"

20–22

19–20

- *over 2-color stranded*
- *using larger needle*
- *before fulling*

You'll need

1 2 **3-4** 5 6

- *Light–medium weight*
  MC • 420 yds
  CC1 • 105 yds
  CC2 • 80 yds
  CC3 • 20 yds
  or 205 yds of one CC
- *non-superwash wool*

I used

- **4mm/US6**
- **4.5mm/US7**
  80cm/32"

- **4.5mm/US7**

- **(optional) 4mm/G**

&

- **2½m/3 yds weighted cotton cord**
- **4 large grommets, grommet tool**
- **2½ × 10" piece of plastic mesh**

KISS PURSE

In preparation for this chapter, I thought about what makes this kind of knitting—2 colors carried and alternating in a round—difficult. Here's my list:

- shaping—any at all;
- a complex chart;
- maintaining an even tension because the chart has large spreads between stitches of the same color or because the number of stitches crowds the knitting onto the needle.

So the Keep-it-simply-stranded purse deals with all of these issues: there is no shaping; the chart is simple, without a large spread between sts of the same color; the number of sts fit comfortably onto a 32" circular needle; and we're going to full it, so idiosyncrasies in tension will disappear. If you've never done this kind of knitting before, here's a first, no-fail project!

Four purses are shown. Two have 1 MC and 3 CC's: one in pale tones on a neutral, gray-brown MC; the other in brights on a neutral, dark green MC. (The brighter one, shown to right, is turned inside-out.) Two other purses are shown, each with only 1 long-space variegated as CC: in one the MC is a neutral, gray-brown; in the other the MC is another long-space variegated.

Notes

1 See *Skills-at-a-glance*, page 228, for long-tail cast-on, e-wrap cast-on, grafting, and 3-needle bind-off. **2** Use smaller needle for Bases and final reverse St st edging.

JO SHARP Classic DK Wool 4 balls in 345 (MC), NORO Kureyon 2 balls in 95 (CC)

CASCADE YARNS Cascade 220 2 skeins in 9405 (MC); 1 skein each 4147 (CC1), 7814 (CC2), and 8885 (CC3)

NORO Kureyon 4 balls in 116 (MC), 2 balls in 102 (CC)

PURSE

Body

1 With MC and long-tail cast-on, cast on 160 sts. Join to work circularly. Place marker to indicate beginning of round.

Work color chart to 10 repeats—80 rows.

See reading charts and knitting 2-color stranded (pages 150 and 156).

Work Purse to 80 rnds.

AT SAME TIME, any time after work measures 2", work Bases.

I like to work the bases early, to carry the yarns in the purse as I work.

2 **First RS base**

With RS facing, count 10 cast-on sts to left of cast-on tail.

*With MC, e-wrap cast on 1 st onto left needle; put needle into right hand, then pick up and k 60 sts along cast-on edge (always going under 2 threads each time); turn needle and e-wrap cast on 1 st—62 sts.

Work St st to 9 rows.*

3 Cut yarn. Put sts onto spare needle.

Second RS base

With RS facing, count 20 cast-on sts of purse to left of section just knit.

Work as from* to* of First RS Base.

Hold 2 needles with RS together, and graft together (or join with 3-needle bind-off).

First WS base

Turn purse to WS, and count 10 cast-on sts to left of cast-on tail.

Work as from * to * of First RS Base.

Cut yarn. Put sts onto spare needle.

Second WS base

Count 20 cast-on sts to left of section just knit.

With WS facing, work as from* to* of First RS Base.

Graft WS bases together.

If you don't like your grafting line, pull it tight—making a seam with no seam allowance.

4 Cut piece of plastic mesh, 2½ × 10". Insert between Bases. Sew open sides of Bases to cast-on edges, sewing 1 row of base to every cast-on st, and turning selvedge edges of Bases and cast-on edges of Purse to inside.

You want to make the inside of this purse as neat as possible, in case you choose to make it the RS.

Upper edge / RSS trim

After 80 rnds, cut CC's. Change to smaller needles, and continue with MC only.

Knit 1 rnd, turn, knit 4 rnds.

Bind off, leaving long tail.

With tail, sew RSS edging down, leaving hole for weighted cord.

Thread 27" of weighted cord through RSS edging; sew cord ends together, then sew hole closed.

Strap

With MC and onto double-pointed needles, cast on 5 sts. K5.

*Without turning work, slip 5 sts to other end of needle.

Pull yarn taut behind, and k5.

Repeat from* until I-cord measures 84".

Thread approx 68" of weighted cord through I-cord. Attach ends of weighted cord with safety pins.

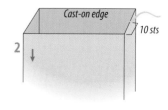

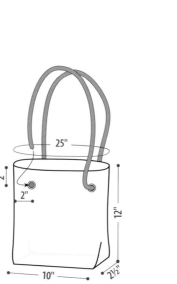

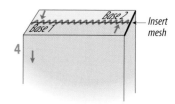

↑ *Direction of knitting*

Kiss chart

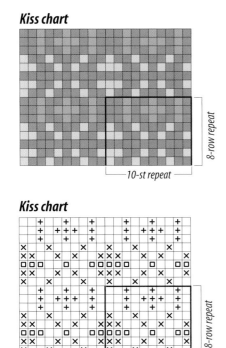

- ■ MC
- ▢ CC1
- ▦ CC2
- ▨ CC3

10-st repeat

8-row repeat

Kiss chart

- ▢ MC
- ☒ CC1
- ⊞ CC2
- ▣ CC3

10-st repeat

8-row repeat

FINISHING

If turning purse to make float side of carries as RS, single crochet (with any color) up color carries (to neaten).

Wash purse and strap in hot water, cold rinse, with soap, twice. Dry in hot dryer.

Use grommet tool to make 4 grommet holes 2" from upper edges and 2" from sides.

Thread I-cord through, with edges of I-cord meeting at inside of purse. Sew weighted cord and I-cord ends closed.

JO SHARP Classic DK wool 4 balls in 345 (MC); 1 ball each in 347 (CC1), 348 (CC2), and 349 (CC3)

EXPERience
- *intermediate*
- *simple stitch pattern*
- *mid-level shaping*
- *mid-level finishing*

C

B | A

LOOSE FIT

Infant 18 months
A *25"* **B** *11½"* **C** *14"*

Woman's *S (M, L, 1X, 2X)*
A *39 (43, 47, 51, 57)"*
B *21 (21½, 22, 22½, 23)"*
C *29 (29½, 30, 31, 31½)"*

10cm/4"

31, 26, 18

21, 16, 12

- *over stockinette stitch*
- *using middle size (main) needles*

You'll need

3 OR **4** OR **5**

Light weight
A • *300 yds*
B • *80 yds*
C • *110 yds*
- *something soft*

Medium weight
A • *590 (660, 740, 825, 900) yds*
B • *160 (180, 200, 225, 250) yds*
C • *115 (130, 145, 160, 180) yds*

Bulky weight
A • *560 (630, 705, 780, 865) yds*
B • *125 (140, 155, 175, 190) yds*
C • *115 (130, 145, 160, 180) yds*

I used

- *3.75mm/US5*
- *4.5mm/US7*
- *6.5mm/US10½*
  any length

- *3.5mm/US4*
- *4.5mm/US7*
- *4mm/US6*
- *5.5mm/US9*
- *6mm/US10*
- *8mm/US11*

- *six 12mm/⅜" (Infant's)*
- *nine 15mm/⅝" (Woman's)*

NORTH-INSPIRED CARDIGAN

There is a wonderful tradition in knitting—often referred to as Icelandic—of sweaters with beautifully-patterned circular yokes. I felt no need to reinvent this tradition but chose, rather, to offer an uncomplicated entrée to it.

The simplest entrée is the 'straight across' version. In the infant's red/orange pattern, the 2-color work is knit straight. You have that option for the woman's red/orange also. But you also have the option, for all woman's garments, to curve the 2-color work—by working short rows. Although these short rows look complex, they are only on the fronts and don't last long.

Colors for the neutrals are a medium gray (main color, A) with light gray (contrast, B) and black (trim, C).

Colors for the bright version are dark violet (trim, C) with its adjacent color, red-violet (main color, A), +the analogous color, red-orange (contrast, B).

Three gauges are shown: 21 sts for infant, 16 sts for neutral version, 12 sts for bright woman's. For the infant's, use numbers for 12-st woman's M unless other instructions are given.

The gray garment was knit to B measurement but then fulled to 1½" shorter.

Notes

1 See *Skills-at-a-glance*, page 228, for SSK, k2tog, yo, SSP, p2tog, lifted inc, bind off in purl, and fulling. **2** The garment is worked in St st (k on RS, p on WS) unless otherwise indicated. **3** The chart does not include edge sts. **4** For 18-months size, work Woman's M, 12-st, unless directed otherwise. **5** When 1 number appears, it applies to all. When 2 numbers appear, the Infant's is first and the Woman's second. When 3 numbers appear, the Infant's is first, 16-st is second, and 12-st is third.

BACK, ALL VERSIONS
RSS edging
With smallest needles and C, cast on 74 (81, 89, 96, 103) or 56 (62, 67, 72, 78) sts.
Work St st for 4 rows, begin with a knit and end with a purl row. Cut C.
Body
Inc row (RS) With A and main (middle size) needle, purl across, increasing evenly in each 9th st—82 (90, 98, 106, 114) or 62 (68, 74, 80, 86) sts.
Work St st in A until piece measures 6" for infant's, 12½ (12, 11½, 11½, 11½)" for woman's. End with a WS row.
SHORTEN OR LENGTHEN HERE
Shape armhole
Infant's only Bind off 4 sts at beginning of next 2 rows, then go to Shape armhole with color pattern.
Woman's only Bind off at beginning of next 2 rows 3 (4, 6, 8, 10) or 3 (3, 5, 7, 9) sts.
Dec row K1, SSK, k to last 3 sts, k2tog, k1.
Repeat Dec row every RS row 1 (4, 6, 8, 10) or 1 (4, 5, 6, 7) times more—72 or 52 sts. End with a WS row.
Shape armhole with color pattern
With smallest needles and C, k 2 rows (without decreasing). With largest needles, A+C, work from chart AT SAME TIME working decreases as follows.
See 2-color stranded knitting and purling (pages 152 and 154) and decreasing in 2-color stranded (page 157).
Dec row K1 in A, SSK, work from chart to last 3 sts, k2tog, k1 in A.
WS row P1 in C, work from chart to last st, p1 in C.
Repeat these last 2 rows 4 (4, 2) times more—50 (62, 46) sts. Continue to work edge sts as written and from chart until charted work measures 2 (2½)", end with a RS row. Cut A. With smallest needles, purl 2 rows in C. Cut C.
Slip sts onto main needle, ready to work a RS row.
With B, work St st until armhole measures 4½" for infant's, 7 (8, 9, 9½, 10)" for woman's.
End with a WS row.
Shape shoulders and back neck
Gauge 16 only Bind off 5 sts at beginning of next of 2 rows.
All sizes Bind off 5 sts at armhole edge, k to 10 sts on right needle. Put next 20 (22, 16) sts on holder.
Turn.
Right shoulder *Bind off 1 st at neck edge twice, AT SAME TIME bind off at armhole edge 4 sts twice.

Left shoulder Return to 15 sts, RS facing.
Knit 1 row.
Bind off 5 sts at armhole edge.
Work as Right shoulder from * to end.
For Infant's, go to Right Front straight.
For gauge 12, choose short row or straight.

RIGHT FRONT, SHORT ROWS
Adult sizes only, gauges 16 (12)
RSS edging
With smallest needles and C, cast on 36 (40, 44, 47, 51) or 29 (32, 35, 37, 40) sts.
Work St st for 4 rows, begin with a knit and end with a purl row. Cut C.

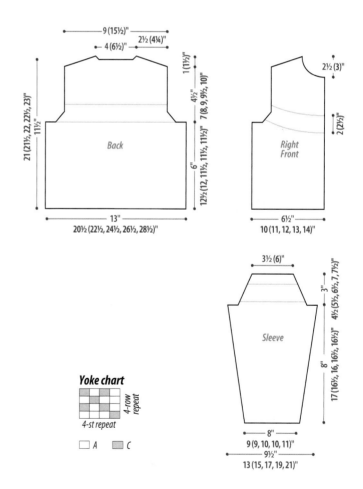

Yoke chart

4-st repeat / 4-row repeat

☐ A ▨ C

Body

Inc row (RS) With A and main needle, purl across, increasing evenly to 40 (44, 48, 52, 56) or 32 (35, 38, 41, 44) sts.

S only Work St st in A to 5 rows shorter than Back length to armhole, end with a RS row.

M (L, 1X, 2X) only Work St st in A to same length as back to armhole, end with a RS row.

Shape armhole + short row, S only

Row 1 (RS) Knit.

Row 2 P23, turn—17 (9) sts left behind (B).

Rows 3 & 5 Yo, knit to end.

Row 4 P15, turn—8B.

Row 6 Bind off 3 sts at beginning of row, p8, turn—4B.

Rows 7 & 9 Yo, knit to last 3 sts, k2tog, k1.

Row 8 P5, turn—2B.

Row 10 P2, turn—2B.

Row 11 Yo, k2. Cut A.

Shape armhole + short-row, M (L, 1X, 2X) only

Bind off at beginning of next row 4 (6, 8, 10) or 3 (5, 7, 9) sts.

M only 40 (32) sts remain.

L (1X, 2X) only: Dec row (RS) Knit to last 3 sts, k2tog, k1. Repeat Dec row every RS row to 40 (32) sts.

M (L, 1X, 2X): Row 1 (RS) Knit to last 3 sts, k2tog, k1.

Row 2 P22, turn—17 (9) sts left behind (B).

Rows 3 & 5 Yo, knit to last 3, k2tog, k1.

Row 4 P13, turn—8B.

Row 6 P8, turn—4B.

Rows 7–11 Work as Rows 7–11 for S size.

Shape armhole with color pattern, all sizes

With smallest needles and C, work as follows.

> At SSK's, you will always slip the k, and you will always k the yo.

Next row (RS) K16 (8), SSK, k7, SSK, k3, SSK, k1, SSK, k1, SSK, k2—35 (27) sts.

Knit 1 row in C.

With largest needles, A+C, work from chart AT SAME TIME working decreases as follows.

Dec row K1 in A, work to last 3 sts, k2tog, k1 in A.

WS row P1 in C, work to last st, p1 in C.

Repeat these last 2 rows 4 (2) times more—30 (24) sts.

Continue to work edge sts as written and from chart to same number of rows as Back, end with a RS row. Cut A.

With smallest needles, purl 2 rows in C. Cut C.

Finish short rows

Slip sts onto main needle, ready to work a RS row. With B, work as follows.

Row 1 K15 (9), turn.

Rows 2, 4, 6, 8, 10 Yo, p to end.

> In k2tog's, you will always knit a stitch and a yo together.

Row 3 K15 (9), k2tog, k5, turn.

Row 5 K21 (15), k2tog, k2, turn.

Row 7 K24 (18), k2tog, k1, turn.

Row 9 K26 (20), k2tog, k1, turn.

Row 11 K28 (22), k2tog, k1, turn.

Continue in A to 7 (5) rows shorter than Back at shoulder, end with a RS row.

Shape neck and shoulder

Bind off at neck edge 5 sts once, 2 sts twice.

Bind off at armhole edge 5 sts twice (once) and then 4 sts twice AT SAME TIME bind off 1 st at neck edges 3 (2) times more.

LEFT FRONT, SHORT ROWS

Work as Right Front to Shape armhole + short-row, end with a WS row.

Shape armhole + short-row, S only

40 (32) sts on needle.

Row 1 (RS) K23, turn—17 (9) B.

Rows 2, 4, 6, 8, 10 Yo, purl to end.

Row 3 K15, turn—8B.

Row 5 Bind off 3 sts at beginning of row, k8, turn—4B.

Row 7 K1, SSK, k3, turn—2B.

Row 9 K1, SSK, turn—2B.

Row 10 Yo, p2.

Shape armhole + short-row, M (L, 1X, 2X) only

Bind off at beginning of next row 4 (6, 8, 10) or 3 (5, 7, 9) sts.

M only 40 (32) sts remain.

L (1X, 2X) only: Dec row (RS) K1, SSK, k to end. Repeat Dec row every RS row to 40 (32) sts.

M (L, 1X, 2X): Row 1 (RS) K1, SSK, k20, turn—17 (9) B.

Rows 2 & 4 Yo, p to end.

Row 3 K1, SSK k11, turn—8B.

Row 5 K1, SSK, k6, turn—4B.

Rows 6–10 Work as Rows 6–10 of S size.

Shape armhole with color pattern

With smallest needles and C, work as follows.

> At the k2tog of the next row, you will knit a stitch and a yo together.

Next row (RS) [K1, k2tog] 3 times, k3, k2tog, k7, k2tog, k to end—35 (27) sts.

Knit 1 row in C.

With largest needles, A+C, work from chart AT SAME TIME working decreases as follows.

Dec row K1 in A, SSK, work to last st, k1 in A.

WS row P1 in C, work to last st, p1 in C.

Repeat these last 2 rows 4 (2) times more—30 (24) sts.

Continue to work edge sts as written and from chart to same number of rows as Back, end with a RS row. Cut A.

With smallest needles, purl 2 rows in C. Cut C.

Finish short rows

With B and main needle, work as follows.

Row 1 (WS) P 15 (9), turn.

Rows 2, 4, 6, 8, 10 Yo, k to end.

In the SSP's, you will always purl a st and a yo together.

Row 3 P 15 (9), SSP, p5, turn.

Row 5 P 21 (15), SSP, p2, turn.

Row 7 P 24 (18), SSP, p1, turn.

Row 9 P 26 (20), SSP, p1, turn.

Row 11 P 28 (22), SSP, p1, turn.

Continue with St st in A to 7 (5) rows shorter than Back at shoulder, end with a WS row.

Shape neck and shoulder

Work as Right Front, but reverse shaping by binding off for neck on RS rows and for shoulder on WS rows.

Go to Sleeves, All Versions.

RIGHT FRONT, STRAIGHT YOKE

Infant's and 12-st only.

RSS edging

With smallest needles and C, cast on 29 (32, 35, 37, 40) sts.

Work St st for 4 rows, begin with a knit and end with a purl row. Cut C.

Body

Inc row (RS) With A and main needles, purl across, increasing evenly to 32 (35, 38, 41, 44) sts.

Work St st in A to same length as back to armhole, end with a RS row.

Shape armhole, Infant's only Bind off 4 sts at beginning of next row, then go to Shape armhole with color pattern.

Woman's only Bind off 3 (3, 5, 7, 9) sts at beginning of next row.

Dec row K1, knit to last 3 sts, k2tog, k1.

Repeat Dec row every RS row 1 (4, 5, 6, 7) times more—27 sts. End with WS row.

Shape armhole with color pattern

With smaller needles and without decreasing, knit 2 rows in C.

With largest needles, A+C, work from chart AT SAME TIME working decreases as follows:

See 2-color stranded knitting and purling (pages 152–154), reading charts (page 156), and decreasing in 2-color stranded (page 157).

Dec row K1 in A, work from chart to last 3 sts, k2tog, k1 in A.

WS row P1 in C, work from chart to last st, p1 in C.

Repeat these last 2 rows 4 (2) times more—26 (24) sts.

Continue to work edge sts as written and from chart to same length as Back, end with a RS row. Cut A.

With smallest needles, p 2 rows in C. Cut C.

Slip sts onto main needle, ready to work a RS row.

With B, work St st until piece is 9 (5) rows shorter than Back armhole, end with a WS row.

Shape neck and shoulder

Bind off at neck edges.

Infant's only 5 sts once, 2 sts twice, 1 st twice.

Woman's only 5 sts once, 2 sts twice.

All sizes Bind off at armhole edge 5 sts once then 4 sts twice AT SAME TIME bind off 1 st at neck edge twice more.

LEFT FRONT, STRAIGHT

Work as Right Front, but reverse shaping as follows:

  • bind off for armhole on a RS row,
  • armhole decreases will be at the beginning of rows (with a k1, then an SSK),
  • neck bind-off's will be at the beginning of WS rows,
  • shoulder bind-off's will be at the beginning of RS rows.

SLEEVES, ALL VERSIONS

RSS edging

With smallest needles and C, cast on 38 or 33 (33, 36, 36, 40) or 24 (24, 27, 27, 31) sts.

Work St st, begin with a knit and end with a purl row, for 4 rows. Cut C.

Body

Inc row (RS) With A and main needles, purl across, increasing evenly in each 9th st to 42 or 36 (36, 40, 40, 44) or 26 (26, 30, 30, 34) sts.

Work St st for 5 more rows.

Inc row (RS) K1, work lifted inc in next st (inc 1), k to last 2 sts, inc 1, knit to end.

Repeat Inc row every 4th row 3 or 7 (11, 13, 17, 19) or 6 (9, 10, 13, 14) times more—50 or 52 (60, 68, 76, 84) or 40 (46, 52, 58, 64) sts.

Work even until Sleeve measures 8" for infant's, 17 (16½, 16, 16½, 16½)" for woman's.
End with a WS row.
SHORTEN OR LENGTHEN HERE

Sleeve cap
Infant's size only Bind off 4 sts at beginning of next 2 rows, then go to Sleeve cap with color pattern.
Woman's size only Bind off at beginning of next 2 rows 3 (4, 6, 8, 10) or 3 (3, 5, 7, 9) sts.
Dec row K1, SSK, k to last 3 sts, k2tog, k1.
Repeat Dec row every RS row 1 (4, 6, 8, 10) or 1 (4, 5, 6, 7) times more—42 or 30 sts. End with WS row.

Sleeve cap with color pattern
With smallest needles and without decreasing, knit 2 rows in C. With largest needles, A+C, work from chart AT SAME TIME working decreases as follows:
Dec row K1 in A, SSK, work to last 3 sts, k2tog, k1 in A.
WS row P1 in C, work to last st, p1 in C.
Repeat last 2 rows while working chart to same number of rows as Back.
End with a RS row. Cut A.
With smallest needles and without decreasing, purl 2 rows in C. Cut C.
Slip sts onto main needle, ready to work a RS row.
With B, work as follows.
Dec rows K1, SSK, k to last 3 sts, k2tog, k1.
Repeat Dec row every RS row until 18 (24, 18) sts remain, end with a WS row.
Bind off at beginning of next 2 rows, 2 sts once then 3 sts once.
Bind off.

FINISHING
Sew shoulder seams.

Collar
Work St st and A.
With RS facing, main needle, pick up and knit as follows:
• 1 st for every bound-off st and 1 st for every 2-row step between bound-off sts at all neck shaping;
• 1 st for every st on holder at Back neck, placing marker at center Back neck—approximately 66 (68, 58) sts.
Work 3 rows even.
Dec row (RS) Knit to 2 sts before right shoulder seam, SSK, k to 3 sts before marker, SSK, k2, k2tog, k to left shoulder seam, k2tog, knit to end.
Work 3 (5) rows even.
Repeat Dec row once.

Work 0 (2) rows even, end with a RS row.
Collar edging
With C (A, C), purl 1 row.
Change to smallest needles and work RSS trim as follows:
Dec row (P8, p2tog) across row.
Knit 1 row, purl 1 row, knit 1 row.
Bind off in purl.

Buttonloops & spaces
See page 139 for a diagram of how these buttonloops and spaces operate. On that sample, they line up; on this one, they alternate down the front of the piece.
On Right Front, mark 6 (9) evenly-spaced spots: 3 (5) spots will be buttonloops, and alternate 3 (4) spots will be spaces.
On Left Front, mark spots that correspond to the 3 (4) spaces.

Left front edging
Row 1 With smallest needles, RS facing, and C, pick up and knit as follows:
• 2 sts for every 3 rows along St st and RSS;
• 1 st for every 1 row along 2-color stranded rows.
Row 2 (WS) Knit.
Row 3, Make buttonloops Purl to first marker, *turn; (WS), cable cast on 6 (5) sts, cable cast on 1 more st BUT, before putting new st onto left needle, bring yarn from back to front between needles; turn, (RS), p1, pass final cast-on st over st just purled, purl to next marker, repeat from* until 3 (4) buttonloops are made; purl to end.
Row 4 Knit.
Row 5 Purl, binding off 6 (5) sts of each buttonloop.
Be careful to bind off the same sts as were cast on.
Row 6 Bind off; sew bound-off edge to seam allowance.
Right front edging
Row 1 With smallest needles and C, pick up and knit as for Left Front AT SAME TIME make spaces as follows:
• stop 1 st before designated spots;
• *turn, cable cast on 1, cable cast on 1 more BUT, before putting new st onto left needle, bring yarn from back to front between needles;
• turn, skip 4 rows over St st or 2 rows over 2-color stranded;
• pick up and knit as directed to next marked spot;
• repeat from* until 3 (4) spaces have been made;
• purl to end.
Work as Rows 2–6 of Left Front.
When sewing down edging across spaces, sew bound-off edge to cast-on row rather than seam allowance.
Sew buttons to correspond to buttonloops.

*Before sewing buttons and to reinforce fabric, you may
  duplicate st 4 sts over which buttons will sit (see page 221).*
Sew Sleeves into armholes.
Sew Sleeve and side seams.
(Optional) Full.

**18 months, page 124: PATONS Look at Me! 2 balls in 6369 (A), 1 ball
each in 6356 (B) and 6370 (C)**
**Woman's M, right: PLYMOUTH YARN Alpaca Boucle 9 balls in 18 (A), 2
balls in 17 (B); CASCADE YARNS Bulky Leisure 1 skein in 8886 (C)**
**Woman's M, page 127: LANA GROSSA Royal Tweed 6 balls in 06 (A), 2
balls each in 07 (B) and 20 (C)**

EXPERience
- *intermediate*
- *mid-level stitch pattern*
- *mid-level shaping*
- *mid-level finishing*

LOOSE FIT

Man's *S (M, L, 1–2X)*
A *40 (44½, 49, 53½, 58)"*
B *22½ (23, 23½, 24, 24½)"*

10cm/4"

28 ▦
29

- *over 2-color pattern*
- *after blocking*

You'll need

1 **2** 3 4 5 6

- *Fine weight*
MC1 • *590 (660, 750, 840, 920)yds*
CC • *320 (360, 410, 460, 500)yds*

I used

- *3 mm/US3*
- *60–70 cm/24–30"*

&

- *separating zipper to fit*

Man's M: BLUE SKY ALPACA Sport Weight
Alpaca 6 balls in 008 (MC), 3 balls in 005 (CC)

IN PRAISE OF DOODLING

One aspect of 2-color stranded knitting that is often (and unfairly) criticized is that it produces horizontal lines, a feature many believe makes us look 'wider.' Without arguing that point, here's a 2-color stranded chart that has strongly vertical lines. It's easy to follow: 1 main color stitch is adjacent to each white vertical, then there are 5 stitches in which most anything can happen. Since it's just a doodle, feel free to make up your own path!

Beyond the obvious difference in color, the man's garment is worked in the round while the woman's is worked flat. Back-and-forth is a departure from traditional 2-color stranded (most often done in the round), but ever since I learned the around-the-neck purl, I find purling 2 colors kinda fun—and very liberating.

The woman's colors are 2 neutrals (off-white, CC, and dark eggplant, MC1) + 1 color (red-orange, MC2). If the eggplant had been lighter, it and the red-orange could be seen as analogous colors. Whatever colors you choose, the lightest and brightest should be in the front and cuffs.

The man's colors are 2 warm browns, a dark for the main color (MC) and a light for the contrast color (CC).

The Vest

Notes
1 See *Skills-at-a-glance*, page 228, for lifted inc, k2tog, and SSK. *2* The vest is worked in St st (k on RS, p on WS) unless otherwise indicated. *3* The vest is knit in one piece and in the round. Armhole and neck shapings are built into the pattern and the pieces are sewn and cut to separate for front and armhole openings: steeks.

BODY
RSS edging
With main color (MC), cast on 213 (237, 261, 285, 309) sts.
Place marker to indicate beginning of rnds.
Working circularly, knit 5 rnds.
Inc rnd Turn work so purl side is facing. With MC, knit 1, work lifted inc (inc 1) in the second st and then every 3rd st—285 (317, 349, 381, 413) sts.
Body
See reading charts (page 156), knitting 2-color stranded (page 150), and steeks (page 158).
Next rnd Change to larger needles, with MC and CC, work Doodling Chart. Begin at right edge, work 8-st repeat and end at left edge.
Work even until piece measures 11 (11½, 12, 12½, 13)".
SHORTEN OR LENGTHEN HERE
Shape armhole
Continuing with Doodling Chart, work 61 (68, 74, 80, 86) sts, bind off next 19 (21, 25, 29, 33) sts, work next 125 (139, 151, 163, 175) sts, bind off next 19 (21, 25, 29, 33) sts, work remaining 61 (68, 74, 80, 86) sts.

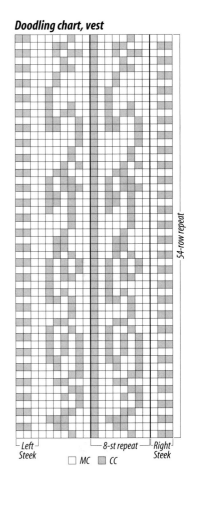

Doodling chart, vest

54-row repeat

Left Steek — 8-st repeat — Right Steek

□ MC ▨ CC

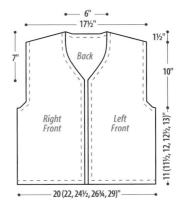

6"
17½"
1½"
7"
Back
10"
Right Front
Left Front
11 (11½, 12, 12½, 13)"
20 (22, 24½, 26¾, 29)"

Yarns continue across armholes to shoulders. See inc's and dec's in 2-color stranded (page 157).

Dec rnd *Work from chart to 5 sts before armhole bind-off, k2tog in MC, work Left Steek Chart over next 3 sts, work Right Steek Chart over next 3 sts, SSK in MC, repeat from* once, work to end.
Repeat Dec rnd every other round 2 (9, 15, 21, 27) times more—58 + 119 + 58 sts remain.

Armhole edges will now begin and end as chart.
When armhole measures 4½", shape V-neck.

Shape V-neck

For some sizes, armhole decs continue.
Yarns continue across V-neck to shoulders.

Dec rnd Work Right Steek Chart over first 3 sts, SSK in MC, work across Right Front, Back and Left Front until 5 sts remain, k2tog in MC, work Left Steek Chart over final 3 sts.
Repeat Dec rnd every other round 19 times more—38 + 119 + 38 sts remain.

Neck edges now begin and end as chart.
Work even until armhole measures 10".

Shape right front shoulder

Work 38 sts.
*Turn, bind off 6, work WS row to Front.
See purling in 2-color stranded (page 154).
Turn, work RS row to armhole.
Repeat from*4 times more.
Bind off 8 sts next RS row.

Shape right shoulder and back neck

Return to remaining sts, RS facing.
Bind off 6 sts at Right Back armhole edge, work to 35 sts on right needle.
Put center 37 sts on holder.
Turn, bind off 1 st at neck edge 3 times
AT SAME TIME bind off 6 sts at armhole edge 4 times more.
Bind off 8 sts next RS row.

Shape left back neck and shoulder

Return to remaining sts, RS facing.
Work 1 RS row over 41 sts.
Turn, bind off 6 sts at armhole edge 5 times, AT SAME TIME bind off 1 st at neck edge 3 times.
Bind off 8 sts next RS row.

Shape left front shoulder

Return to 38 sts, RS facing.

Bind off 6 sts at armhole edge 5 times.
Bind off 8 sts next RS row.

FINISHING

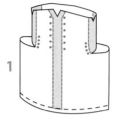

Armhole and front openings

See sewing and cutting, page 159.
In 1st and 2nd steek sts from armhole and Front edges, sew 2–3 tight lines of machine stitching on either side of cut line.
Cut along cut lines.
Sew shoulder seams.

Armhole edgings

On all cut edges, pick up and knit 1 full stitch past sewing line.

This leaves one MC stitch clear around entire edge.
With RS facing and CC, pick up and knit around armhole edges as follows:
- 3 sts for every 4 bound-off sts at underarm;
- 2 sts for every 3 rows on cut edges.

Next rnd With CC, purl.
Next rnd With MC, knit.
Following rnds With MC, purl.
Bind off when edging is wide enough to cover seam allowance.
Sew bind-off edge to seam allowance.

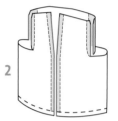

Front and neck edging

Work 1 full stitch past sewing line.
With RS facing and CC, pick up and knit around Front and neck edge as follows:
- 2 sts from RSS edgings;
- 2 sts for every 3 rows along straight Front edges;
- at points of V's, work (k1, yo, k1) in same stitch;
- 3 sts for every 4 rows along diagonal Front edges;
- 7 sts around curve of Back neck shaping;
- work (k4, k2tog) across sts on holder.

Next row With CC, knit.
Next row With MC, knit.
Following rows With MC, purl RS rows, knit WS rows.
Bind off when edging is wide enough to cover seam allowances. Sew bind-off edge to seam allowance.
Sew zipper to Fronts, from lower edges to points of V.

EXPERIEnce
- *advanced intermediate*
- *mid-level stitch pattern*
- *mid-level shaping*
- *mid-level finishing*

LOOSE FIT

Woman's S (M, L, 1–2X)
A 40 (44½, 49, 54)"
B 20½ (21½, 22, 22½)"
C 31½ (32, 32½, 33)"

10cm/4"

28
26

- *over 2-color pattern*
- *using larger needles*
- *after blocking*

You'll need

1 **2** 3 4 5 6

- *Fine weight*
MC1 • *650 (720, 860, 930) yds*
CC • *540 (600, 700, 780) yds*
MC2 • *325 (360, 425, 470) yds*

I used

- *3.25 mm/US3*
- *3.5mm/US4*

- *fourteen 13mm/½", round or 19mm/¾", rectangular*

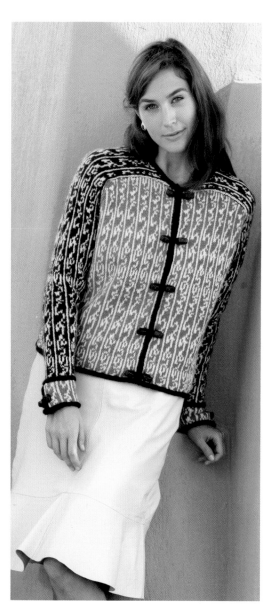

The Jacket

Notes
1 See *Skills-at-a-glance*, page 228, for SSK, k2tog, p2tog, SSP, and lifted inc. *2* The jacket is worked in St st (k on RS, p on WS) unless otherwise indicated. *3* These pieces are worked flat, back-and-forth in rows, not in the round.

BACK
RSS edging
With smaller needles and dark (MC1), cast on 104 (116, 129, 142) sts.
Work 6 rows St st, beginning with a knit and ending with a purl row.
Inc row (WS) Purl across, increase every 4 sts—129 (145, 161, 177) sts.
Body
Change to larger needles. With MC1 and CC, work Chart B. Start at right edge, work 8-st repeat, end at left edge. When piece measures 12½ (12½, 12, 12)", end with a WS row.
SHORTEN OR LENGTHEN HERE
Shape Armhole
Bind off 5 (7, 9, 11) sts at beginning of next 2 rows.
Read down to your size before working next 4 rows.
RS dec row K1 CC, k1 MC1, SSK, work to last 4 sts, k2tog, k2 in MC1.
See inc's and dec's (page 157).
RS row K1 CC, k1 MC1, work to last 2 sts, k2 MC1.
WS dec row P1 CC, p1 MC1, p2tog, work to last 4 sts, SSP, p2 MC1.
WS row P1 CC, p1 MC1, work to last 2 sts, p2 MC1.
S size only *Work [RS dec row, WS row] 3 times, then work (RS row, WS row) once; repeat from* to 93 sts.
M size only Work [RS dec row, WS row] to 93 sts.
L size only *Work [RS dec row, WS row] 8 times, then work [RS dec row, WS dec row] once; repeat from* to 93 sts.
1X–2X size only *Work [RS dec row, WS row] 4 times, then work [RS dec row, WS dec row] once; repeat from* to 93 sts.
All sizes End with a WS row.
Armhole will measure 4¾ (5½, 6½, 7½)".